What to Wear
to Show Off
Your Assets

your
perfect
fit

What to Do to
Tone Up Your
Trouble Spots

Paige Adams-Geller and Ashley Borden
with Zibby Right

New York Chicago San Francisco Lisbon London Madrid Mexico City
Milan New Delhi San Juan Seoul Singapore Sydney Toronto

The *McGraw·Hill* Companies

Library if Congress Cataloging-in-Publication Data

Adams-Geller, Paige.
    Your perfect fit : what to wear to show off your assets, what to do to tone up your
trouble spots / Paige Adams-Geller, Ashley Borden, with Zibby Right.
        p.   cm.
    ISBN 978-0-07-150271-9
    1. Physical fitness for women.   2. Clothing and dress.   3. Women's clothing.
    4. Fashion.   I. Borden, Ashley.   II. Right, Zibby.   III. Title.

GV482.A33   2007
613.7'045—dc22   2007026782

1 2 3 4 5 6 7 8 9 10 11 12 13 14 15 16 17 18 19 20   DOC/DOC   0 9 8 7

ISBN   978-0-07-150271-9
MHID   0-07-150271-8

Interior design by Monica Baziuk
Illustrations by Lauren Riback

McGraw-Hill books are available at special quantity discounts to use as premiums and
sales promotions, or for use in corporate training programs. For more information, please
write to the Director of Special Sales, Professional Publishing, McGraw-Hill, Two Penn
Plaza, New York, NY 10121-2298. Or contact your local bookstore.

This book is printed on acid-free paper.

This book is dedicated to those of you who thought being a fashion expert was reserved for fashion editors and clothing designers. May you find your goddess within and remember that we all have a little glamour in us . . . we just need to wear it properly.

—PAIGE

This book is dedicated to my momma, Carol Borden. You raised me with perfect balance: you never judged, and you always believed in my vision. I am so lucky to be your daughter.

—ASHLEY

Contents

Acknowledgments

I would like to say thank you to my husband for being my partner in life and in this crazy but fabulous world of fashion. To my amazing stepchildren, Allie and Jon, for keeping me hip. To Elizabeth Gamza for guiding me down the path of success. To my mother who taught me from an early age that class was in my attitude and in my wardrobe. To my father who taught me to give everything 110 percent. For my brother, Troy, and my sister, Konnie, for being my biggest fans. I want to thank my dear, dear friend Wendy for so much more than I can say. To Lisa, Mikki, Kimberly, and Jules for believing in my heart. Thanks to Missy for keeping me in working order. To Lacie for keeping me sane and more organized than I ever thought possible and for being such a soothing presence in my life. I sincerely thank my CEOs (canine executive officers) Taffy and Ashley for their unconditional love and snuggles. I am so happy to have had the opportunity to write this book with Ashley Borden; she is truly an expert. A special thank you to Dana Sarbeck for her support and for knowing that Ashley and I would be a perfect fit. Thanks to Lauren Riback for bringing my tips to life. To everyone at McGraw-Hill and Harvey Klinger, Inc. To Johanna Bowman and Sara Crowe in particular. Thank you to Zibby for coming along with us for this ride, all while carrying twins. And thanks to the twins for waiting to be born until the book was finished.

—*Paige*

Dana Sarbeck: you are the world's most unbelievable publicist. You are my foundation and voice of reason. You inspire me with your dedication to animals, and your word is always *gold*. I honor our friendship and love you like family. Karl List: my mentor and a brilliant educator. I am honored to have trained and studied with you. Thank you for all of your knowledge and dedication. You have made me the trainer I am today. My family: Rossy, my pure love and rock. Joelstir, my dad, thank you for your unconditional love and helpful feedback. Cris, my brother, thank you for always keeping me grounded. Kevin Anderson, Esq: you rock as an attorney *and* a person. Thank you for your patience, believing in me, and being part of my dream team. Matt Mahowald: you opened my eyes to a new life with food. I have learned so much from you—thank you. The book team: Zibby Right, Sara Crowe, Johanna Bowman, and Lauren Riback. This book could not have come alive without all of your help and hard work. Thank you! Paige Adams-Geller: thank you for your honesty and willingness to reveal yourself. You are an inspiration, and I am thankful to have you as a book partner. Christina Aguilera: many, many thanks—I am forever grateful. My wonderful clients at the gym: I am proud to be your trainer and to have each of you as a client. Thank you for all of your hard work! Tamara: the best workout partner, thank you for keeping my mind and body strong.

—*Ashley*

Introduction

I want you to love your body, feel comfortable in your skin, and be comfortable in your jeans (genes).

—PAIGE ADAMS-GELLER

How many times, when getting dressed for a big night out, have you looked at yourself critically in the mirror and wished for a different body? Perhaps you've stood there, in the first of many outfits that will soon lie discarded on your bed, twisting and turning to check out every angle, convinced that you look awful, that everyone at the party will look more put-together, thinner, and better looking than you. Or maybe it's a good day—your skinny jeans fit!—and you think you don't look half bad. But still, what you wouldn't give for a few extra inches off your hips!

Your eyes flutter to the celebrity magazine lying open on your desk and the actress on a red carpet, dressed up for a night out. You fantasize about how easy life would be if you looked like any of the models and actresses in the pictures. Their lives must be amazing. They don't have multiple pairs of jeans in bigger and bigger sizes depending on the week. They probably just know how to dress, what to eat, how to act. As you yank off your top to try on the next option, you think again: why can't that be me?

We know exactly how you feel. Looking and feeling good takes some work—although not as much as you might think. We help those celebs look that picture perfect, and we want to help you. We want to share our style, fitness, and health secrets to give you the strategies you can use every day to feel and look confident and fit. The tips we've picked up from the trenches of image-obsessed Hollywood life will empower you, giving you the tools to know that you don't have to be a supermodel to have a fun night out; in fact, you'd have the best time just being you.

We know all too well how tough it is to have a healthy body image. Both of us have struggled with poor self-esteem and at one point have had serious eating disorders. It used to take us forever to get dressed to go out; it all depended on what our eating had been like that day. If we'd been bingeing or starving, we might not have gone out at all. But if we had to, we used to disguise ourselves as much as possible, wearing jeans without a button at the top, loose-waist pants with a looser top, or even all black, just to disappear. Getting ready was always an ordeal because it brought our appearance front and center; we tried to compensate for how much we disliked our bodies by paying extra attention to our hair, skin, and makeup, but that never worked. No matter what, we'd both get dressed and undressed and then dressed again and end up with eight thousand piles of clothes on the floor. Sound familiar?

As the symptoms of our eating disorders grew more pronounced—the puffy face and awful skin from bulimia; the shame, isolation, eating in secret and lack of energy from anorexia—our body images grew more and more distorted: it was only us, our mirrors, and our magazines.

We used to look at pictures of celebrities and think, "Look at their thighs and look at how huge mine are," or "I'm so badly proportioned compared to them." The childhood taunts would play on repeat in our heads, tormenting us. We constantly compared ourselves to our friends and felt we never measured up.

PAIGE

As a former Miss California and fashion model, I was constantly being evaluated by how I looked. Every time I told someone what I did for a living, I felt like it was a sham, that I didn't look good enough to be a model. The more people focused on my outside appearance, the less I felt like anyone knew who I really was. It got worse and worse until finally I realized I needed to seek help. I hated myself.

Even comments from outsiders were damaging, from well-intentioned friends telling us to lose weight to our former boyfriends' snide comments about what they wished our bodies looked like. It seemed like we were evaluated at every turn and all of our positive attributes—our intelligence, wit, humor—were just ignored. Because we had such low self-esteem, we listened to all the negatives and never paid attention to all the positives about us. We grew more and more self-conscious, not out of vanity, but from feeling the need to control something in our lives. At least when our stomachs were flat or we liked our outfits, we felt we had accomplished something, that we were finally in control.

Finally, at different stages in our lives, we both sought treatment for our eating disorders through twelve-step programs and hospital inpatient centers. Thank goodness.

Before, hating ourselves felt like a full-time job. Now, post-treatment, we finally feel great about who we are. Even going out is completely different. We wear clothes we feel comfortable in, and we don't spend time obsessing about our bodies; we're focused on the people we're with. It took a lot of time and work, but we realized that it's not how we look but how we *feel* that matters. We're not prisoners in our own skin anymore, and our self-esteem isn't based on what we look like—it's based on what we have to say.

ASHLEY

*I*t wasn't until I spent two whole weeks hiding inside my house, bingeing and purging seven times a day, that I realized I was completely self-destructing. I had to find a way out. I remember going downstairs at age eighteen and telling my mother that I thought I was going to kill myself. I went into treatment the next day. I like to say that I suffered from "terminal uniqueness"; I didn't think anyone could possibly understand what I was going through. I started going to Overeaters Anonymous, and it changed my life. I finally felt centered, and after two years, I was firmly in recovery, although I'll never say "recovered."

It wasn't until we heard real models and actresses talking about how every little thing is airbrushed that we started to realize how much time we'd wasted hoping for an ideal that didn't even exist. All media images can be (and most are!) digitally enhanced to make stars look leaner or larger depending on the news angle, from tabloid photos to music videos. Meanwhile, every celebrity thinks there's some celebrity weight-loss secret floating around that only she doesn't know. The truth is that there is no secret. It takes the right combination of food and fitness to reshape your body, whether or not you're from Hollywood. Just because someone's famous doesn't mean she's naturally thin; she has to work at it just like everyone else—and sometimes pay the price for her success.

We've dedicated our lives to helping other women feel good about themselves too; we want everyone to be spared the agony of self-loathing. Paige created a line of denim that flatters every body type, so women can feel comfortable in their jeans. Ashley became a fitness and lifestyle consultant helping women get the bodies they want and deserve.

We wrote this book to share our tips and secrets with more of you. Feeling confident comes from the inside, but part of feeling great comes from knowing you're dressed in the most flattering way possible. We've given you tons of fashion tips for each body part that women obsess about the most. Whether you're struggling to hide your bum or desperate to flaunt those oft-hidden shoulders, we have easy-to-execute fashion tips. We also provide specific exercises to help you improve and feel even better about the parts of your body that may need a little extra help. In just minutes, our easy-to-follow, effective strength-training moves will tone your hidden zones into areas you'll want to flaunt. Ashley's S.O.S. Food Plan is another healthy and sustainable way to help get you the body you always wanted.

Don't do as we did; do as we wish we had done. By following our hard-earned advice about fashion, fitness, nutrition, and well-being, we guarantee you'll feel fabulous in your jeans—and your genes.

Getting Started

Setting Your Fashion and Fitness Foundation

*Y*ou're a total package. You can't separate your inside from your outside when both are equally important. We want to help you put your best foot—and shoe—forward to look and feel your best, so we're offering our expert fitness *and* fashion advice. Our fitness moves make you feel good from the inside out, while our fashion advice takes how you feel and projects it to the world. When you combine exercising, eating well, and dressing smart, you can improve your life and boost your self-confidence. Our tips will equip you with the foundation you need to build the life, body, and look you want.

Adopting an entirely new fitness and fashion philosophy can feel overwhelming, so we've divided our tips by body part, offering you a very user-friendly guide. You can cut to the chase and tackle specific body issues or problems and then expand your search for a full-body transformation. Like everything else in life, it's better to take it one step at a time.

This chapter gives you the tools you need to get the most out of this book, but the fun is yet to come! As you read past this chapter, you'll learn how to tone specific areas of your body in just days. You'll also learn how to dress the best for your body type while maintaining your style and individuality. Fashion is a great way to self-express—and to cover your flaws and enhance your assets. Finally, the S.O.S. Food Plan will give you the foundation for a lean, livable lifestyle.

When you start taking care of yourself and staying true to who you are, your kindness and confidence will emanate to the world around you. So dive in!

DRESSING UP

Nothing can replace the sensation of looking and feeling smashing in a fabulous outfit. Having great-fitting clothes that flatter your body type is a woman's dream. Shopping for them, on the other hand, can be a nightmare. Your size seems to fluctuate with the stock market. A store can make your day when you fit into a small size, but how quickly your good mood ends when you walk into the store next door and find you've gone up two sizes. And that's when it's *not* that time of the month. The whole experience is enough to make you swear off shopping ever again—almost. Don't let it.

Size *Really* Doesn't Matter

The best way to feel great about your body is to wear clothes that really fit. A lot of designers have started "vanity sizing," making everyone think they're a smaller size than they used to be. Why not—who doesn't like fitting into a smaller size? But the trend is troubling because now there are no standards across the industry. You've probably noticed that designers don't always play by the rules.

Buy whatever fits, and ignore the sizes. Rip the tags out if you really can't stand it, but don't buy based on falsified numbers. Take home the clothes that fit you comfortably, and then go back to your trusted brands. Or visit a reputable tailor and have your clothes altered for you; it doesn't have to *cost* a million bucks to look like a million bucks.

PAIGE'S TIP: ▷ If you can't find the right pair of pants, ask for help from the salespeople and try to walk into the store knowing your waist and hip dimensions—it'll save time and help you find the perfect fit.

Diamonds Are a Girl's Best Friend

Knowing what body type you have is helpful when dressing right for your frame. Of course, all bodies are unique. They're precious, beautiful, and deserve to be treasured and respected—just like diamonds. Here are five common body types that represent the rare gems you truly are.

Emerald Cut ("Boyish," "H-Body Type," "Ruler")

The following are the characteristics of the emerald-cut body (Figure 1.1):

- Your upper and lower body are proportionate.
- Your bust, hips, and waist are in a straight line and have similar measurements.

You're lucky for the following reasons:

*Figure 1.1
The emerald-cut
body shape.*

- People think you work out like crazy even when you don't; you're just genetically on the leaner side.
- Your legs are one of your greatest assets.
- You tend to gain weight all over—proportionately. When you put on that little extra on vacation or over the holidays, no one can tell.

Your biggest challenge is giving your body some shape and curves if you so desire. You can accentuate your shoulders and hips and create more of a waistline by cinching clothes in at the waist.

Celebrities with this body type include Gwyneth Paltrow, Cameron Diaz, Kate Moss, and Kate Hudson.

Fashion Dos
- Blouses with shoulder details, such as slightly puffed sleeves or lightly padded shoulders
- A-line skirts

PAIGE SAYS: ✂ The shape of an A-line garment resembles the letter A. The width at the top of the garment is more fitted and gently flares out to a greater width at the bottom. This shape mostly applies to skirts, dresses, coats, and tops.

- Higher-waisted pants with small waists and wide leg openings
- Belts cinched in at the waist (Figure 1.2)
- Miniskirts
- Tops with ruffles or ruching at the bustline (Figure 1.2)

PAIGE SAYS: ✂ Ruching can be a trim in which lace, silk, or ribbon is gathered to create ruffling. It can also apply to large gathered areas in a garment that create a rippling or pleating effect.

Figure 1.2.
Do wear tops with
ruffles and belts
cinched in at the waist.

Figure 1.3.
Don't wear sheath
dresses with no shape.

- Empire-waist tops that push you up and create a more rounded bust shape
- Halter tops
- Low-rise fitted jeans
- Wrap dresses or tops that tie at the waist

Fashion Don'ts
- Sheath tops or dresses with no shape (Figure 1.3)
- Trouser-style pants that are loose and full and fall straight from the waist
- Boxy T-shirts and button-downs
- Vertical lines from head to toe
- Loose, baggy clothes that make you look boyish—unless that's your style and you don't mind not seeing some curves

Teardrop Diamond ("Bell-Shaped," "A-Shaped," "Triangular")

Characteristics of the teardrop diamond shape include the following (Figure 1.4):

- Your shoulders are smaller than your hips.
- You have a small upper body with longer legs.
- You tend to carry weight around your bottom and hips and always gain weight first in the lower half of your body.

You're lucky for the following reasons:

- You usually have great, lean arms and a narrow back.
- You are likely to have a small waist and a flat stomach.
- Since you have the most common body type, it's easiest to find clothes that fit you.

Figure 1.4.
The teardrop body shape.

Your biggest challenge is trying to balance out your upper and lower body.

Celebrities with this body type include Jennifer Lopez, Beyoncé, and Shakira.

Fashion Dos

- Darker colors on the bottom
- Jeans or pants with a slight boot cut to even out your proportions
- Skinny jeans with longer tunics on top (Figure 1.5)
- Scarves, accessories, and jewelry that accentuate the upper body
- Empire-waist tops that drape softly over the hips

Figure 1.5.
Do wear skinny jeans
with longer tunics.

Figure 1.6.
Don't wear belts
around your hips.

- Tops with interesting shoulder details to draw attention upward
- Blazers and fitted blouses that lightly skim the body

Fashion Don'ts
- Low-slung belts or scarves around your hips; they only draw attention to your wider areas (Figure 1.6)
- Large prints on your bottom half
- Heavy fabrics, such as wool, corduroy, or velvet, that make you look fuller on the bottom
- Clingy dresses or tight-fitting clothes from head to toe
- Skimpy tops with A-line skirts (wear a top with eye-catching details)
- Large or elaborate pocket detailing on the front or back of your pants, especially around the hip area

Kissing Trillions ("Hourglass," "Figure Eights")

Characteristics of the kissing trillions body include the following (Figure 1.7):

- Your bust and hips are about the same size.
- Your waist is much smaller.

You're lucky for the following reasons:

- You have a voluptuous bosom and beautiful curves. (This is the *it* in the "if you've got it, flaunt it" shape.)
- You tend to gain weight proportionately.
- You're usually considered the feminine ideal (i.e., the elusive "36-24-36").

Your biggest challenge is elongating your body. Celebrities with your body type include Halle Berry, Selma Hayek, and Scarlett Johansson.

Figure 1.7.
The kissing trillions
body shape.

Fashion Dos
- Monochromatic outfits that flatter from head to toe
- Plunging necklines

PAIGE SAYS: ⟿ *Monochromatic* refers to dressing in one color from head to toe.

- V-necks with a wider opening
- Scoop-neck tops and dresses (Figure 1.8)

PAIGE SAYS: ⟿ A scoop neck is a front or back neckline of any width or depth that has a rounded, soft curved shape.

- Sweetheart necklines

PAIGE SAYS: ⟿ A sweetheart neck is a front neckline that resembles the shape of a heart.

- Three-quarter-length jackets that have shape in the waist and a single-button closure
- Off-the-shoulder tops and dresses

Figure 1.8.
Do wear scoop-neck dresses and three-quarter-length jackets.

Figure 1.9.
Don't wear strapless dresses.

- Boot-cut pants and jeans with a classic rise
- Pencil skirts

Fashion Don'ts

- Strapless dresses or tops with no strap support—look for spaghetti straps at least (Figure 1.9)
- High necklines, like crew-neck tops
- Double-breasted jackets
- Bold prints on the top and bottom
- Miniskirts
- Cropped pants

Heart-Shape Solitaire ("Swimmer's Body," "V-Shape," "Funnel")

Characteristics of the heart-shape solitaire include the following (Figure 1.10):

- You have broad shoulders and a much narrower waist and hips.
- You tend to carry weight around your middle.

You're lucky for the following reasons:

- You usually have amazing legs and beautiful broad shoulders.
- You're often considered buxom—people pay a ton of money for that look!

Your biggest challenge is drawing attention away from your middle and evening out your proportions.

Celebrities with your body type include Renée Zellweger, Elizabeth Hurley, and Keira Knightley.

Fashion Dos

- A-line pants or skirts with a slight flare
- Tops that skim your stomach area and aren't too clingy (Figure 1.11)

Figure 1.10.
The heart-shape body.

- Slightly tapered button-down shirts
- Lighter colors on the bottom
- V-neck tops with deep V-necks

PAIGE SAYS: ⊳ A V-neck is a front or back neckline that is shaped like the letter V.

- A-line miniskirts
- Sleeveless tops

Fashion Don'ts
- Blouses with too many ruffles or details on the upper body
- Shoulder pads
- Clingy fabrics that accentuate your middle
- Smaller spaghetti straps (Figure 1.12)

Figure 1.11.
Do wear tops that skim
the stomach area.

Figure 1.12.
Don't wear leggings or clingy,
spaghetti-strap tops.

- Leggings (unless you pair them with a long top that extends beneath your derriere) (Figure 1.12)
- Strapless tops (unless you wear an A-line shape on the bottom)

Diamond Shape ("Apple")

Characteristics of the diamond-shaped body include the following (Figure 1.13):

- You have narrow shoulders and slim hips.
- Your most full, round area is your middle.

  You're lucky for the following reason:

- You usually have long, lean limbs, especially shapely arms and flaunt-worthy legs.

  Your biggest challenge is broadening your shoulders and hips to help create the illusion of a smaller waistline, without over-compensating and looking larger.

  Celebrities with your body type include Christina Ricci and Kelly Osbourne.

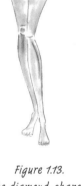

Figure 1.13.
The diamond-shaped
body.

Fashion Dos

- Knee-length skirts that are tulip shaped or have ruffles on the bottom
- Long tunic-style tops in soft and drapey fabrics over skinny jeans or leggings (Figure 1.14)
- Three-quarter-length trench coats with wide belts
- Any button-down blouse with slightly padded shoulders or slightly puffed sleeves
- Tailored, structured blazers in navy or black with a colored or printed top underneath
- Colorful jewelry around the neckline
- Trousers or jeans with a wider waistband
- Boot-cut or wider-leg pants
- Empire-waist tops with bell sleeves

PAIGE SAYS: An empire waistline sits right below the bust-line, lending the garment a very high-waisted effect.

Fashion Don'ts

- Dresses or tops that are too clingy (Figure 1.15)
- Pants or skirts with heavy pleating or gathering around the waist
- Wide, elastic cinch belts that cut the waistline in half and create stomach bulges
- Blouses with narrow shoulders or large bold prints
- Pants with too low a rise
- Shirts and jackets with heavy detailing in the midsection, such as kangaroo or patch pockets

Figure 1.14.
Do wear tunic tops
over skinny jeans.

Figure 1.15.
Don't wear dresses that are clingy
or that gather around the waist.

PAIGE SAYS: ⤳ A kangaroo pocket is an extra-large front pocket placed on the front of a garment near your stomach (where a kangaroo's pouch would be).

GENERAL FASHION ADVICE

Knowing *what* to wear is one thing. Knowing *how* to wear it is another. Although we'll give you oodles of tips for enhancing various outfits, we can't resist sharing a few general guidelines right off the bat. Many derive from our personal pet peeves, but all have been honed through our years of working in the Hollywood trenches. We think you'll agree: they just make sense! Keep the following dos and don'ts in mind as you go through each body-part chapter. Although not all will apply to *your* body (everyone is unique), choose the ones that emphasize your most positive features:

- Please wear underwear when you wear short skirts. One false move, and you're showing off more than your style.
- Wear strapless only when you know there's no chance of wardrobe malfunction.
- Be cautious about wearing skirts with slits that go up too far.
- Try not to wear stockings and undergarments that need constant adjustment. Make sure they fit before you leave the house.
- Wear jeans that fit—nothing destroys a sexy pair of jeans more than butt cleavage.
- Low-rise jeans look better with slightly longer tops.
- When you wear leggings, cover up your derriere with a longer top or dress.
- Wear one trend at a time; wearing multiple trends can be overpowering.
- Try not to wear head-to-toe denim or leather.
- Be aware of overpowering logo display.
- Buy only shoes you can walk in.
- When you're at a wedding or an event honoring someone else, try to take the backseat, fashion-wise.
- Most important of all, learn to love your body!

SETTING YOUR FITNESS FOUNDATION

Now that you've learned the basics of dressing right, it's time to address your body's basic fitness needs. Working out is critically important. Physiologically, training helps prevent osteoporosis by creating more density in your bones. You'll be less prone to injury and will experience fewer aches and pains. Doing cardio exercise keeps cardiovascular (heart) disease at bay and gives you more energy. In fact, training paired with eating right can help reduce your blood pressure and cholesterol and make you more in control of your health. You'll find yourself standing up taller as your posture improves.

Training also improves your mood. Working out produces a chemical release of endorphins in your brain, which helps combat depression and anxiety. It also makes you more conscious of and connected to your body, which can lead to making better choices about food intake and lifestyle. Once you start a fitness program, you'll be more likely to participate in activities outside of the gym, like going hiking with a girlfriend instead of just meeting for drinks and appetizers.

Not only that, but your body will begin to change. Doing weight-bearing exercise creates more muscle in your body. The more muscle you have, the higher your metabolism becomes. Your body burns fat and replaces it with muscle, giving you a leaner look, since a muscular body takes up less space.

In this book we give you the tried-and-true tools to maintain a lean, livable lifestyle. Think of this chapter as your warm-up. In subsequent chapters, we'll tackle various body parts, cumulatively giving you a total body workout.

Workout Wardrobe Essentials

Having great-fitting workout clothes is the first step to adopting a fitness regime. Dressing the part really inspires your workout—the more committed you *look*, the more motivated you'll *feel*. Fitness attire doesn't have to cost an arm and a leg. Here are our suggestions for what to buy (or pull out from the depths of your closet) for getting started.

- **Black tights or yoga pants:** The right bottoms can prevent chafing and hold everything in place. Wear Dri-Fit or Dri-Weave fabric, or wickable fabrics, which means they keep the moisture away from your skin. Buy two pairs so you can alternate.

> **ASHLEY'S TIP:** When you're trying on workout pants in a store, bend over and look in the mirror. If you can see anything you shouldn't, forget it!

- **Socks:** White and black no-show running socks are most flattering on your ankles and lengthen out your body. Two pairs of each are ideal. Buy the appropriate socks for the sport that you're doing. There's a reason why they're called running socks: the extra padding on the balls of your feet helps cushion your feet as you apply pressure downward.

- **Sports bras:** Look for wickable fabrics (e.g., Dri-Fit and Dri-Weave) instead of plain cotton, which can chafe when damp. Make sure the sports bra doesn't constrict your breathing; you should be able to comfortably inhale and exhale without feeling your rib cage is squashed. If you're a C-cup or larger, opt for a more traditional style compression top that comes in regular bra sizes (not small, medium, and large). If you're a B-cup or smaller, opt for a racerback or T-back styles in size small or medium. Always have two sports bras to interchange.

- **Lingerie bag:** Wash your sports bras and running socks in a special lingerie bag (available at major department stores) to make them last longer.

- **Sneakers:** Go to a specialty running store to have your sneakers fitted (see the sidebar, "Buying the Right Sneakers for You"), and replace them when the tread of your shoe gets worn down. Time takes away from the structural integrity of the shoe, so if your sneaks have been sitting in the closet for two years, donate them and buy a new pair.

- **Tank tops:** Wear comfortable, loose-fitting tanks that don't chafe your armpits. Make sure the armholes aren't too tight.

ASHLEY'S TIP: If you want your tummy to look a little flatter, layer two tank tops on top of each other. The tank underneath should hit just below your hip bones. The tank on top should end just a little bit above them.

- **A comfortable, oversized hoodie:** A cozy, hooded sweatshirt is the perfect thing to toss on over your tank before and after a workout.

- **Bandana:** Wear one to keep your lovely mane out of the way when you're working out.

- **A large water bottle:** Don't leave home without it.

Warming Up

OK, you're all dressed and ready to start setting your new fitness foundation. Anyone who applies the tools consistently can have a fabulously toned body—very exciting! But we must immediately quell one huge misconception that is floating around. A lot of women fear that if they start lifting weights, they'll become bulky and look like the Terminator. Ha! Not a chance. The amount of training and eating one has to do to get to that level of fitness is mind-blowing and certainly won't happen by accident. Also,

BUYING THE RIGHT SNEAKERS FOR YOU

*I*f possible, go to a specialty running store so someone can perform a "gait analysis." This involves analyzing the way that you walk before fitting you in the appropriate pair of shoes. If you don't have access to a specialist, step on the hard floor when you get out of the shower and see what shape your foot makes on the ground. You want to see a crescent of dry floor—that means you have high or low arches. But if you can see your entire footprint on the floor, then your arches have collapsed and you need significantly more arch support in a sneaker.

most women don't have the amount of testosterone needed to really bulk up like a man.

Here's a simple way to make sure you're lifting the right amount for your goals:

- To build muscle size and strength, lift heavy weights (80 to 100 percent of the maximum you can lift) and do few repetitions, only 3 to 8 reps per set.
- To tone and create a lean body, lift lighter weights (50 to 75 percent of your maximum) and do more repetitions, 10 to 20 reps.

So now that you're no longer afraid of morphing into Ahnold, a couple of other things apart from training will help your body look and feel toned and gorgeous. First, your percentage of body fat (which you can have tested at your local fitness center) determines how well you can see results. Don't hide your killer muscles under a useless layer of fat. Find your body mass index (BMI) if you don't know your body fat percentage (see Appendix A). Doing "Smart Cardio," which means cardiovascular exercise for sixty minutes in your fat-burning zone, reduces your body fat by elevating your heart rate to a point at which it burns calories and fat. Any exercise that gets your heart rate up for a sustained period of time, from martial arts and tennis to running and biking, helps shed that cloak of bloat and lets all your hard work shine through.

Finally, we have to address the effects of food. Eating in a healthy, conscious, and timely manner helps reduce body fat, gives you more energy to live your life, and vastly improves your physique.

Finding Your Target Heart Rate

Working out at your target heart rate ensures that your metabolism is in fat-burning mode.

1. Determine your *maximum* heart rate (MHR): 220 − your age. For example, if you are thirty years old, your MHR would be 220 − 30 = 190.

2. Determine your *target* heart rate, which is when your metabolism is in aerobic, or fat-burning, mode. Your target heart rate is between 65 to 80 percent of your MHR (Step 1).

   Step 1 × 0.65 = low end of range (in the preceding example: 190 × 0.65 = 123.5)

   Step 1 × 0.8 = high end of range (in the preceding example: 190 × 0.80 = 152)

Sometimes you'll vary the intensity of your workouts outside of fat-burning mode. Follow these guidelines for varying intensities:

Moderate (Slightly Below Fat-Burning Zone)
Step 1 × 0.5 = low end of range
Step 1 × 0.6 = high end of range

Moderately Difficult (Getting in the Zone)
Step 1 × 0.6 = low end of range
Step 1 × 0.7 = high end of range

Challenging (in the Sweet Spot)
Step 1 × 0.7 = low end of range
Step 1 × 0.8 = high end of range

Very Tough (at the Top End of the Zone)
Step 1 × 0.8 =low end of range
Step 1 × 0.9 = high end of range

Almost Impossible to Sustain (Above the Zone, Now Anaerobic)
Step 1 × 0.9 = low end of range
Step 1 × 0.99 = high end of range

There are two types of exercise: aerobic and anaerobic. *Anaerobic* means "without air." When you're sprinting or doing heavy lifting, you probably find it tough to breathe. Because your body can't use oxygen as energy, it starts to produce lactic acid, which causes muscle fatigue during such activity.

Aerobic exercise is typically done at a lower intensity and is much easier to sustain for longer periods of time (think jogging versus sprinting). Your body does use oxygen for energy and therefore can keep on going and burning fat. While both types of exercise are important for overall fitness, when you're doing our recommended Smart Cardio, you should opt for an intensity level that is challenging but not impossible.

When doing cardio, monitor your heart rate with either a heart-rate monitor or by taking your pulse for six seconds and then multiplying it by 10.

Help! How Do I Find My Pulse?

Lightly place the tips of your index and middle fingers on the inside of your wrist, just under the base of your thumb. (Your thumb has its own pulse, so don't use it to find the pulse elsewhere.) Feel the beating? Congratulations! You've found your pulse. Now see how many beats you feel in six seconds. Then multiply that number by 10. That's your current heart rate. Compare it to the ranges you've computed for your age, and see how you're doing.

Finding Your Perceived Level of Exertion

Another good way to tell how hard you're working, without any math, is to measure your perceived level of exertion.

Use this scale from 1 to 10:

1–2: I can speak very easily.
3–4: I can speak, but it's getting a little more difficult.
5–6: Carrying on a conversation is now taking a lot of effort.
7–8: I . . . can't . . . speak . . . without . . . panting . . . .
9–10: Gasping . . . for . . . air . . . help!

Ten Measurements to Track Your Progress

If you follow the exercises in this book and the S.O.S. Food Plan, your body will start to respond within two days. You'll look and feel less bloated, your clothes will feel larger around your

waistline, and you'll have a lot more energy. But a tape measure is the only accurate tool to let you know how your body is
changing. Recording small changes all over your body tells the
whole story of what's going on with your workouts and food. The
measurements track your progress efficiently and are much less
emotionally charged than the number on the scale. Take your
measurements every two weeks to really measure your progress.

Stand with feet hip-width apart, arms at your sides, eyes
straight ahead. Wear only undies and the same sports bra when
taking measurements, and be sure to bend over and scoop your
boobs into the bra before starting. If possible, ask your partner,
trainer, or trusted friend to take the measurements for you—
they'll be much more accurate.

1. Neck: Measure the circumference of your neck in the middle
around your Adam's apple.

2. Chest: Run the tape measure around the middle of your back
at your nipple line.

3. Waist: Measure the smallest part of your waist that you see in
the mirror.

4. Tummy: Wrap the tape around your hips in line with your belly
button.

5. Hips: Find the widest part of your hips. First, measure how
many inches down it is from your belly button (so you can find
it each time). Then go around your hips all the way around and
over your tush.

6. Arms, relaxed: Let your arms hang by your sides. Take your
right hand and spread your fingers as far apart as they will go.
Place your right-hand pinky on the inside elbow crease of your
left arm, stretching your thumb up as close as possible to your
armpit. Note where your middle finger is. Take the measurement
around your relaxed arm there. Repeat with right and left arms.
Remember, your arm on the dominant side is always bigger.

7. Arms, flexed: Repeat the preceding arm measurement method
on your right and left arms with your biceps flexed.

ASHLEY'S TIP: To flex your muscle, make a fist with your thumb inside your fingers against the palm of your hand. Close your forearm up to your biceps, and squeeze as if you were crushing a nut.

8. **Quads:** Measure your quads right under the crease of your tush and across your thighs.

9. **Thighs:** Measure your lower thighs three inches above the top of your kneecap.

10. **Calves:** Put your thumb inside the back of your knee, and spread your pinky as far down your calf as you can. Measure at your middle finger.

Also, before starting the food plan, get a cholesterol blood panel at your doctor's office so you can track all the positive changes occurring on the inside, too. Some weeks you may not lose inches, but your cholesterol may have gone down—a huge coup!

Training Guidelines

The next eight chapters contain fitness moves targeted to specific body parts from your shoulders to your toes.

Full-Body Workout

For a comprehensive, full-body workout, you need to mix and match the moves. Target two body parts during each workout. Aim for three training sessions per week. To help tone your body, start each workout session with one series of shoulder moves to warm up and do one abs move in between sets.

Each body part chapter offers a series of moves for toning that body part. For some body parts, the series of moves must be followed exactly as written—sequentially. When you train these areas, repeat the series two to three times in the same order.

- Shoulders
- Butt

- Hips
- Thighs
- Calves

Sample Workout 1: Hips and Butt

Shoulder series warm-up

Hips series, butt series

One abs move

Hips series, butt series

One abs move

For other body parts, you can select some or all of the moves in any order you like. They do not have to be done sequentially. When you train these areas, pick at least two to three moves for each area, alternating between the two body parts:

- Arms
- Back
- Abs

Sample Workout 2: Arms and Back

Shoulder series warm-up

One arms (biceps) move, one back move, one abs move

One arms (biceps) move, one back move, one abs move

A second arms (triceps) move, a second back move, a second abs move

A second arms (triceps) move, a second back move, a second abs move

ASHLEY'S TIP: To make this sample workout more challenging, repeat these moves twice.

Feel free to mix and match all body parts, but if the shoulders or hips are one of the two, start with them.

Sample Workout 3: Calves and Back

Shoulder series warm-up

Calves series, one back move, a second back move

One abs move

Calves series, one back move, a second back move

One abs move

Over the course of the week, you should train six body parts in three training sessions. Start the next week with the two body parts you didn't get to in the first week.

Targeted Workout

If you want to target a specific body part, do 2 to 3 sets of the moves outlined in that chapter (see individual chapters), two to three times a week.

Now that you're fully versed in the basics, it's time to get to work. Each chapter contains valuable tools to help you build your fitness and fashion foundation, so sit back, relax, and enjoy all our hard-earned advice!

Armed with Confidence

The Biceps and Triceps of Your Dreams

It's amazing how much we take our arms for granted. Those of us who don't like our arms look at them critically in photographs and think, "My arms look like huge loaves of bread!" or "See how skinny and weak they look?" We rarely stop to appreciate just how vital—and beautiful—our arms truly are. Arms give us strength. They protect us, and they allow us to move, lift, drive, and eat. Their sheer grace, those long limbs extending from the sculptural human form, is often overlooked.

With so much emphasis on arms these days, it's hard not to be a little self-conscious. Celebrity body types have morphed from Marilyn Monroe to Madonna as fitness-conscious stars like Sheryl Crow and Jennifer Aniston flaunt their toned biceps and triceps in classic gowns instead of covering them. Smaller, flirtier tops such as silk camisoles and sleeveless garments are everywhere. Should we wear these tops or resist the right to bare arms?

We used to think that genetics alone determined that we wouldn't have red-carpet-worthy biceps. Now we've learned that although genetics always plays a role in our body types, it is no excuse. Anyone can have sculpted, toned arms—it just takes the right food, moves, and lifestyle choices and attitudes. Even celebrities work extra hard to battle the under-arm-wobblies. Body fat doesn't care who you are. There's no shortcut to amazing arms, but by doing the right combination of weight lifting and cardio—and by limiting body fat all over to see those hard-earned results—anyone can look their absolute best.

Even if you're not quite ready for Oscar night, we have dozens of fashion tips for turning your arms into your greatest asset.

ARMED AND DANGEROUS: DRESSING FOR SUCCESS

Shopping for flattering tops can be overwhelming. What would look better: a tank top, camisole, long-sleeve blouse, a T-shirt with cap sleeves, or even a blazer? With so many cuts and styles, it's no wonder that many of us end up wearing the occasional "don't." Here are a few best bets for whatever type of arms you have. Remember, all of our bodies have amazing assets. Stop for a moment and think about what your best body part is. Your flat abs, your thick and luminous hair, maybe your gorgeous fingernails? If your arms aren't your favorite, accentuate whatever you like most.

If you think your arms are your greatest asset, *do* wear:

• **Vests:** Pair vests with a tiny tank top underneath—or even wear it on its own. Vests are such a great way to show off your arms without seeming masculine.

> **PAIGE'S TIP:** Wearing a three-snap leather vest with nothing underneath or with just a tiny tank can make you feel like a rock star.

• **Tank tops:** This fashion staple looks amazing and has a unique way of enhancing arms. Racerback tanks are particularly sexy. By cutting the angles close to your neck and shoulders and angling them down beneath your arms, tank tops really highlight the arm's form. Just be careful that the cut of the armhole and shoulders is flattering on *your* body. If the straps are too long and droopy or the armholes are too big, find another style. Don't be afraid to alter the sleeves. Sometimes a few quick stitches are all it takes to turn a "don't" into a "do."

> **PAIGE SAYS:** A racerback is a style of shirt or dress in which the back armholes are cut in, forming an X-shape in the middle of the back and leaving the shoulder blades exposed.

- **Spaghetti straps:** Perfectly placed straps are great for showing off arms. However, watch out for the proportion of spaghetti straps to your body. If the straps are too tiny, your body can seem larger.

- **Cap-sleeve tees:** These fitted tops cut arms off at just the right point for maximum accentuation. Try not to let the sleeves get too tight and cut off your circulation (ouch!), and make sure they're not too long or you'll miss all the benefits.

- **Silk camisoles:** These flirty, luxurious tops show off great arms and shoulders.

- **Angel sleeves:** Sleeves that billow loose off the shoulder and are accented by lace and chiffon edges are very flattering for biceps and triceps (Figure 2.1).

> **PAIGE SAYS:** Angel sleeves are long and flowing. Sometimes these sleeves have slits from the shoulder to the sleeve opening that expose the arm.

If you think your arms are your greatest asset, *don't* wear:

- **Muscle shirts:** They're not flattering to anyone, and they make your arms look less than delicate.

> **PAIGE SAYS:** A muscle shirt is a sleeveless, knitted shirt that fits tightly on the body and is banded around the armhole.

Figure 2.1.
Angel sleeves flatter biceps and triceps.

If you feel that you have thicker arms, *do* wear:

- **Long sleeves:** The length of the sleeve makes arms look longer and leaner, no matter what.

- **Three-quarter-length sleeves:** We girls tend to have lovely forearms and wrists. Cutting off the sleeve mid-forearm accentuates the forearms instead of drawing attention to the upper arms, creating a longer look and highlighting a more appropriate asset.

- **Cuffs with lace:** Having an attention-grabbing fabric at the end of your sleeves takes the eye away from your arms and toward your hands.

- **Wider straps:** Instead of donning thin, spaghetti straps, which can make larger arms look even bigger, find wider straps that are proportionate to your body.

- **Tailored button-down shirts:** You always look smart in a nicely cut, tailored shirt that flatters your arms, elbows, and wrists.

PAIGE'S TIP: Try not to wear a button-down that ends above your elbow, unless it has a slightly puffed sleeve. If the shorter sleeve is too straight, it can make you look a little dowdy and frumpy—and we don't want that!

- **Baseball shirts without shoulder seams:** Raglan-sleeve tops (i.e., having seams from the neck and underarm only) in a fitted T-shirt style are a very attractive look (Figure 2.2).

PAIGE SAYS: A raglan sleeve starts at your neckline and is set in by seams that slant upward from the front and back underarm. The seams can be straight or slightly curved. Think baseball jersey.

- **Blazers:** They're awesome! They always look good with any kind of button-down shirt for a corporate look or over a sexy top or T-shirt for a night out. They give you a polished, finished look and can disguise the arm area nicely.

Figure 2.2. Raglan sleeves look smashing on thicker arms.

- **Wrap dresses:** Dresses are great for the arms, especially sleeveless wrap dresses that are so stunning on a figure. Simply use the same principles (dos and don'ts) for picking a top as for picking the style of dress.

If you feel that you have thicker arms, *don't* wear:

• **Shirts with tight bands around the sleeves:** Avoid sleeves with elastic around the edges or cap sleeves that dig into your skin. Otherwise your arms will look and feel like your ankles do when you wear too tight a sock that leaves a mark for hours afterward! Cutting into your skin only makes it look like you have extra flesh.

• **Tight tops in light colors:** Doing so will just bring more attention to your arms.

• **T-shirts with wide, unshaped arms:** Why bother? They look frumpy and unflattering. Go for something fitted and young looking.

• **Anything that cuts too tightly under your arms:** If a top gives you some "chicken flesh" between your chest and your armpit, get rid of it!

If you feel that you have extra-long arms, three-quarter-length sleeves put the focus on the sleeves and not the arms. Other interesting sleeve shapes also distract attention. If the sleeves are too short, push them up over your elbows. The worst is when the cuff is too short. Keep long-sleeve, fitted black tops at arm's length: they'll certainly highlight your long limbs.

If you feel that your arms are too short, short sleeves are your safest bet. Bell sleeves, which are bell-bottoms for the arms, lengthen arms, as do kimono sleeves, which hit below the elbow and then get looser to show off your forearms. But try not to wear anything that covers your hands; three-quarter-length sleeves might look like a perfect fit on you.

A Few Other Arm Insecurities

If you have really *pale, porcelain skin,* don't shy away from sleeveless tops. Flaunt your paler arms: stars like Julianne Moore and Drew Barrymore show off their whiter skin with grace, wearing colors that accentuate their other features, such as their eyes. If you're not ready to bare all, you can always consider using a

ACCESSORIZE, DAHLING

*T*o bring even more focus to your hands and wrists, wear beautiful rings and bracelets. Pile on bangles, and wear attention-getting jewelry. But avoid tight arm cuffs for thicker arms. Purses can also direct attention to the right places. If you're proud of your arms, carry a clutch tight to your body to show off those babies. If not, carry larger purses such as hobo and shoulder bags, especially if you have no definition between your shoulders and your arms. Classic wraps and pashminas are other great ways to cover up while keeping nice and warm; they can disguise almost any body part you're unhappy with, and they look fabulous to boot.

trusted brand-name self-tanner that blends in nicely, doesn't give you a funky color, and doesn't smell bad.

If your arms have *embarrassing bumps or blemishes* on them, start treating your arms like you do your face. Use all the same products. Make sure to shower after a trip to the gym, and try not to wear wool if you tend to get sweaty. Use a shower scrub to do away with dead skin, and apply a body-glowing shimmer after for a beautiful sheen and soft, silky skin.

If you have *tattoos or birthmarks* you absolutely must disguise, use a cover-up cosmetic that blends in without rubbing off. But don't feel embarrassed to express your individuality. Every mark on your body makes you special; don't feel the need to hide what makes you *you*.

If your arms are a little *too hairy* for prime time, try not to succumb to the temptation of shaving them. The hair grows back and looks awful. Talk to your dermatologist about laser removal or bleaching options for long-term happiness.

AN INVITATION TO THE GUN SHOW

Developing killer arms can be a piece of cake if you follow the exercises in this chapter. Even moderate lifting three times a week can transform your upper arms from saggy to staggering. Now get off the couch, and get started!

ASHLEY'S TIP: Don't pump iron if you're about to go out to a big event. The lifting temporarily increases the size of your muscles, because of a buildup of lactic acid, but you want your muscles to appear flat and not even slightly swollen, right? Instead, try to do an hour of fat-burning cardio. After cardio, your legs might look and feel slightly bigger from the increased blood flow. Don't worry: leave at least an hour of time before the big event and they'll subside.

You'll need:

- A medium-resistance, hollow tubing band with handles
- Dumbbells: 3, 5, or 8 pounds

  How much weight should you use?

- For biceps moves, start out with 5-pound dumbbells. For triceps, start with 3-pound dumbbells.
- If you can easily do 15 reps with perfect form, go up in weight. Keeping your excellent form, gradually add weight until you can just do 15 reps.
- Try not to compromise your form for extra weight or extra reps. Resist the urge to compare yourself to anyone else. Lift the amount that's right for you and not for some stranger across the room.

The Warm-Up

Walk for five minutes on the treadmill at a level 3 to 5 incline at 3 to 4 miles per hour (mph). If you don't have access to a treadmill, walk briskly outside at exertion level 7 for five minutes (see "Finding Your Perceived Level of Exertion" in Chapter 1).

Biceps and Triceps Stretch and Fire

Start with these two exercises to warm up the appropriate muscles.

Biceps: Turn and Squeeze -

1. Bend your forearms toward the biceps with your hands relaxed (Figure 2.3).
2. Squeeze your biceps while keeping hands relaxed. (Be sure not to do a death grip on it.) Turn your pinkies toward your thumbs, palms facing away from your body.

   ASHLEY SAYS: A death grip is when you excessively squeeze the weight you're using. You want to feel your muscles contracting, not your hand going numb from gripping the life out of the weight!

3. Continue to squeeze for 5 seconds. Extend your arms back down with your fingertips reaching toward the floor. Repeat 3 times.

Figure 2.3.
Biceps turn
and squeeze.

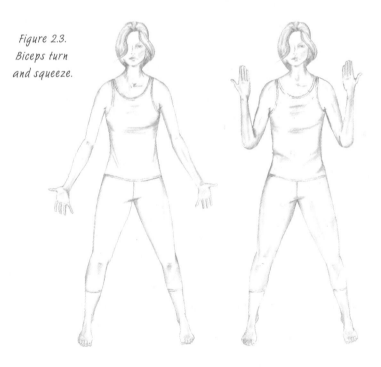

Triceps: Stop Signs

1. Start in athletic stance: set your spine with your arms at your sides; spread your fingertips and reach them toward the floor (Figure 2.4).

Figure 2.4.
Triceps stop signs.
Press through the heel
of your hand.

ASHLEY SAYS: Athletic stance is an active setup stance in which you're setting your energy and rooting yourself into the ground (Figure 2.5). Stand with your feet just beyond hip-width apart, feet facing forward so you can't see your heels in the mirror. The weight of your foot is balanced between your big toe and second toe and the back edge of your heel. Raise the arches of your feet as if you have a marble underneath them, and keep your glutes tight. Bend your knees slightly and push them out to the sides, holding your belly in.

2. Pull your palms back and push through the heels of your hands to fire (contract) your triceps; slowly raise both arms to shoulder height, and keep pressing through the heels of your hands and contracting your triceps. Hold for 5 seconds.

3. While pressing through the heels of your hands, slowly press your arms down to your sides. Repeat 3 times.

Training Guidelines

1. Alternate one of the biceps exercises and one of the triceps exercises that follow. Do 3 sets of each. Alternate a second biceps exercise and triceps exercise. Do 3 sets of each. Alternate a third biceps exercise and a triceps exercise. Do 3 sets of each. For example:

   - Standing double-arm hammer curls with a twist
   - Triceps kickbacks

     Repeat for 3 sets.

   - Tray biceps with band
   - Corn triceps

     Repeat for 3 sets.

   - Side curls
   - Triceps hammers with band

     Repeat for 3 sets.

Figure 2.5.
Athletic stance.

2. Do this workout (with any moves you like) two to three times a week.

   ASHLEY'S TIP: Do the shoulder series (see Chapter 3) first to warm up your upper body.

The Moves

To make any of the following moves more challenging and to work on your balance, do them standing on one leg or even on one leg balanced on a folded-up yoga mat.

Biceps

Standing Double-Arm Hammer Curls with a Twist ------

1. Start in athletic stance, and set your spine. Holding a dumbbell in each hand, extend your arms down by your sides with your palms facing in. Contract your biceps.

   ASHLEY SAYS: "Set your spine" is a setup command meaning "eyes on the horizon, mouth closed, tongue pressed at the front of your teeth, jaw pulled back and up."

2. Bring your forearms up so the dumbbells are at shoulder height perpendicular to your body. At top, rotate your wrists with your pinkies turning inward and palms facing your body, and squeeze your biceps like you're crushing a nut in your elbow (Figure 2.6). Release down, and repeat 10 times.

   ASHLEY'S TIP: Rotating your wrists inward squeezes the head of your biceps, giving them a more chiseled look.

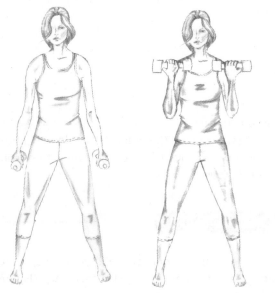

Figure 2.6. Standing double-arm hammer curls, like squeezing a nut in your elbow.

Tray Biceps with Band -------------------------------

1. Start in athletic stance. Put the middle of the exercise band under the arches of your feet, holding each handle with one hand. Set your spine, and press your shoulder blades down.

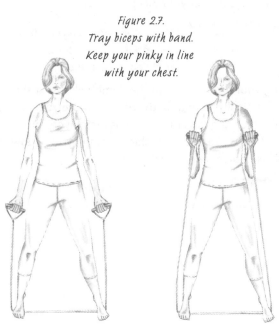

Figure 2.7.
Tray biceps with band.
Keep your pinky in line
with your chest.

2.   Bring your forearms up to a tray position so your pinkies are in line with your chest (Figure 2.7), parallel to the floor at a 90-degree angle to your body. Hold. Release down again to starting position, and repeat 10 times.

Reverse Curls with Dumbbells -------------------------

1. Start in athletic stance, and set your spine. Put your arms at your sides, palms facing back and one dumbbell in each hand (Figure 2.8). (Again, no death grip.)

Figure 2.8.
Reverse curls
with dumbbells—
no death grip!

2. Curl the weight up, raising your elbows slightly so the dumbbells are at shoulder height. Squeeze at the top.
3. Release and bring your arms down to your sides. Repeat 10 times.

Side Curls

1. Start in athletic stance, and set your spine. Hold your arms at your sides, one dumbbell in each hand and palms facing away from your body. Keep your shoulders down, away from your ears, and elbows in place.
2. Curl the weights up to your shoulders as if you're holding down a scarf over your head (Figure 2.9). Squeeze.

Figure 2.9.
Side curls. Curl weight
as if holding a scarf
over your head.

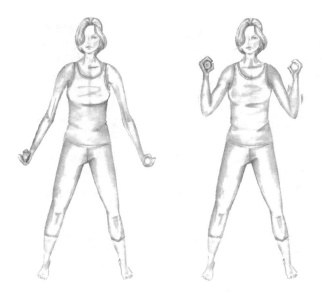

3. Release down to your sides, and repeat 10 times.

Triceps

Triceps Kickbacks --

1. Start in athletic stance, holding a dumbbell in each hand, arms at your sides.
2. Bend your upper body over so your back is flat, parallel to the ground like an ironing board (Figure 2.10), and extend your arms along your upper body. Keep your head in line with your spine.
3. Push your knuckles toward the wall behind you, arms fully extended, and squeeze triceps. Release and bend your elbows. Repeat 10 times.

ASHLEY'S TIP: Don't roll your shoulders forward; keep chest open and shoulders back so you will work the top part of your triceps.

Figure 2.10.
Triceps kickbacks. Keep
your back as flat as
an ironing board.

Corn Triceps --

1. Lie down on a bench or on the floor with your knees bent and feet flat on the ground, and contract your abs. Hold one dumbbell with both hands as if it were a piece of corn on the cob, and extend your arms straight up so the dumbbell is centered over your chest.
2. Holding in your abs, bend at your elbows and bring your forearms back over your head toward the ground behind you (Figure 2.11). Pull your shoulders down to the ground as you pull belly button in toward the bench.

Figure 2.11.
Corn triceps. Hold the dumbbell
as if it is corn on the cob.

3. Bring the dumbbell back directly over your chest, keeping your arms extended above you. Repeat 10 times.

Triceps Hammers with Band ----------------------------

1. Sit on a bench or chair with your feet flat on the floor; contract your abs and keep your shoulders down and your back straight.
2. Take a band behind your back. Hold the top of the band lightly with one arm over your shoulder and the bottom of the band lightly with your other arm around your lower back as if you were using a towel to dry off after a shower (Figure 2.12). Keep the band completely parallel with your body.

Figure 2.12. Triceps hammers with band. Hold the band as if you're drying your back with a towel.

3. Keeping your bottom arm in place with your palm facing out, extend your top arm toward the ceiling as far as it can go and squeeze your triceps. Release down, and repeat 10 times.

Modified Cobra Push-Ups ------------------------------

1. Lie facedown on a mat with your palms flat on the ground next to your armpits, elbows raised up toward the ceiling. Keep your toes pointed and tops of your feet on the ground. Push your shoulders away from your ears.
2. Keeping your knees on the ground and your arms close to your body, push up through your palms. Raise your upper body in a cobra position (Figure 2.13). Slowly release down, and repeat 5 times.

Figure 2.13.
Modified cobra push-ups.
Raise and lower your
body like a cobra.

Want to Make This a Full-Body Cardio Workout?

After the warm-up, do one set of biceps exercises and one set of triceps exercises. Then do one of the following cardio moves. Repeat the whole series twice. For maximum benefit, do this workout three times a week.

Cardio Blast Suggestions

Adding cardio to your workout raises your heart rate and helps burn more calories throughout.

Athletic Jumping Jacks -------------------------------

1. Stand with your feet hip-width apart, holding a dumbbell in each hand. Bend your elbows, and raise your hands by your shoulders, palms facing in.
2. Jump your feet out wide as you press the dumbbells up overhead in a "V for victory" position (Figure 2.14). Hop your feet back in, and bring your lower arms back to the starting position. Repeat 10 times.

Figure 2.14.
Athletic jumping jacks.
Make a "V for victory"
sign with your arms.

Jump Squats --

1. Lie facedown on the ground in the plank position: hands directly under your shoulders, legs together, and feet flexed so you're raised up on your toes (Figure 2.15). Contract your abs.
2. Jump forward so your legs are on either side of your hands in a leapfrog position. Stand up.
3. Squat as if you were sitting down in a chair, arms extended in front of you. Return to plank position. Repeat 10 times.

Figure 2.15. Jump squats. Start in plank position, jump into leapfrog, stand, and squat in a chair position.

AN ARMY OF ONE

Remember, anyone can improve her arms. Consistency is key for getting the results you want. You should feel empowered knowing that toned, strong biceps and triceps are within your reach. All you have to do is practice these moves, and soon you'll be fighting for the chance to show off your guns. So get fired up, and be all that you can be!

Secrets to Stunning Shoulders

Toning Your Upper Torso for Great Effect

Shoulders are very important. Not only do toned shoulders help frame our bodies and make us look beautiful, but they're also essential in making us the strong, capable women we are. Plus, what's more feminine than the gentle slope of a woman's shoulder where it meets her neck? It's time to start working this critical body part.

NO SHRUGS ABOUT IT: HOW TO DRESS FOR YOUR SHOULDERS

Dressing to accentuate different shoulder types can be easy as pie (OK, a piece of fruit), but the first step is to know what type of shoulders you have: narrow, wide, average, sloped, or square.

In order to assess your body type, take the following two measurements:

- **Shoulder width:** Measure across your back from shoulder to shoulder, stopping where the arm and shoulder bone meet.
- **Hip width:** Measure all the way around your hips at the top of your hipbone. Divide by 2. The result is the width of your hips.

You have *broad* shoulders if your shoulder width is more than two inches wider than your hip width. You have *narrow* shoulders if your shoulder width is more than two inches smaller than your hip width. You have *average* shoulders if your shoulder width is within two inches of your hip width.

No matter how wide or narrow your shoulders are, their shape can range from sloped to square. You have *sloped* shoulders if your shoulders slope significantly downward from the base of your neck. You have *average shape* shoulders if your shoulders have a slight slope to them starting at the base of the neck. You have *square* shoulders if the end of the shoulder is even with the base of the neck.

Now let's get you dressed, girl!

If you have narrow shoulders, *do* wear:

- **Halter tops:** Thin-strapped halters (e.g., the straps of a bikini top) look fantastic on narrow shoulders. Traditional or empire-waist styles look great, but stick with something with a nice A-line shape and avoid anything that skirts out too much.

PAIGE'S TIP: Pair the halter with a straight skirt or skinny jeans to make your shoulders appear wider and more balanced in relation to your hips.

- **Halter dresses:** The skirt should be straight— only slightly A-line—so the focus can stay on the breadth of your shoulders (Figure 3.1).

- **Pea coats and double-breasted blazers with wide or shawl collars:** The width around the neck makes the shoulders look wider.

Figure 3.1. For narrow shoulders, do wear halter dresses.

- **Dolman sleeves:** Long sweaters with dropped shoulder sleeves that are wide and drapey at the armholes are hip and look cool (Figure 3.2). V-neck sweaters with dolman sleeves are great. Long tunic sweaters with loose sleeves over leggings or skinny jeans also make the shoulders look broader. If you want to wear something fuller on the bottom, try a shorter dolman sleeve top that hits at the waist and has a band around the bottom.

PAIGE SAYS: A dolman sleeve has very low armholes and is loose, giving a billowing effect. This sleeve shape can also apply to coats and sweaters.

- **Tops with gathering and ruching around the shoulders:** These types of details draw attention to the neckline and create the illusion of greater length between the shoulders.

- **Slightly padded shoulders:** Beware of the 1980s—we said "slightly"! If you're wearing a blazer, make sure there's only a hint of a shoulder pad and that the seam is at the broadest part of your shoulders (Figure 3.3). If the pads make you look too big and broad, you'll end up looking like a football player, or if you have a tiny waist, like a professional weight lifter.

Figure 3.2.
Dolman sleeves look great on narrow shoulders.

- **Off-the-shoulder tops:** Anything that dips off your shoulders with either a straight or sweetheart neckline accentuates your shoulders, making you look regal, princesslike, and oh-so-feminine.

- **Horizontal stripes:** You're the only ones who can get away with these. Enjoy.

PAIGE'S TIP: Buy a dazzling long necklace that falls into your cleavage area. Collared chokers bring the focus back up to your neck and face, as does anything glitzy and sparkly around your face such as earrings or hair accessories. Even a dash of bright red lipstick can do the trick by taking attention away from any insecurity you may have.

Figure 3.3.
Go for blazers with slightly padded shoulders.

- **Scarves:** Wear a scarf around the very top of your shoulders, and tie it right in front of your bustline in an open sailor knot.

If you have broad shoulders, *do* wear:

- **Halter tops:** Pair these with something wide on the bottom; donning a traditional A-line skirt or loose-fitting pants will make your shoulders seem more diminutive. Wider strap halters are best; they leave less shoulder exposed. A deep V-neck also elongates the shoulder-to-waist portion of your upper body.

- **White on the bottom:** Don't be afraid to wear white. For you, it's a plus, plus, plus. Wearing a white A-line skirt or wide-leg pants will even you out by bringing the eye down and not across those shoulders.

- **Strapless dresses:** Wide shoulders look gorgeous in strapless gowns. Wear one that has an A-line or wider skirt to even out your proportions.

- **Peplum blazers:** Take a style tip from the 1940s, and pair a peplum blazer with a teeny-tiny belt around your waist over either a straight skirt for a tailored look or wide-leg pants à la Katharine Hepburn.

> **PAIGE SAYS:** A peplum is a flared ruffle or extension of the bodice that is attached to or comes below the waistline of a jacket, dress, or blouse.

- **Plunging necklines:** This style, much like the recommended halter-top version, shows off your neck and bosom and distracts the eye from your blades.

- **Boatneck (ballerina neck) tops:** The crescent-shaped neckline, unlike a basic crew neck (which can look boxy on broader shoulders), helps soften the line between your shoulders. This shape also draws attention away from the shoulder area by exposing the oh-so-feminine collarbone.

- **Scarves:** To make broad shoulders a little more dainty, tie a great printed, colored scarf around your neck. Wear it loose like you would with a heavy coat: in one little loose knot around your cleavage, in a V-shape.

If you have broad shoulders, *don't* wear:

- **Dolman sleeves:** Since they widen your shoulders, they won't flatter your broader top.

- **Shawls:** These cozy tops just aren't the most flattering option for you. Stick to sweaters and jackets that enhance your frame.

- **Puffed sleeves:** Again, these types of sleeves take the eye to exactly the wrong place.

- **Shoulder pads:** Leave these babies in the 1980s.

- **Horizontal stripes:** Just say no.

> **PAIGE'S TIP:** You should be proud of having broad shoulders! Having broad shoulders is one thing that runway models crave because it makes their hips and waist look smaller. You look amazing in all sorts of gowns and on the red carpet—just look at Halle Berry, Renée Zellweger, Jennifer Garner, and even Kate Hudson!

If you have sloped shoulders, *do* wear:

- **Tailored blouses:** A tiny bit of a puffed or angel sleeve can give more shape to your upper torso.

- **Blazers with shoulder pads:** Not too big a pad—you don't want to give Joan Collins a run for her money.

- **Wide collars:** They camouflage your shoulder shape by drawing attention to the neckline.

- **Cap sleeves:** These add definition to sloped shoulders by cutting off just below the point at which the shoulder naturally angles.

- **Military-style shirts and jackets with epaulets:** Adding bulk to the top of the shoulder area helps counteract the steady slope. Epaulets are tabs or cloth pads that button at the shoulder.

If you have sloped shoulders, *don't* wear:

- **Halter tops:** These are not recommended; they enhance the shape of the shoulders.

HAIR "DOS" TO ENHANCE
YOUR SHOULDERS

*H*ow you cut your hair can affect your shoulder physique. If you have *broad* shoulders, try avoiding short, pixie haircuts. Those of you with *narrow* shoulders can totally get away with short haircuts, so experiment! If you love your shoulders, updos are a beautiful way to show off your neck and shoulders—and all the hard work you've put into getting them!

• **Clingy knit tops:** Be careful about wearing something too soft and loose like a knit top, which gives no shape to your shoulders.

• **Off-the-shoulder tops:** This style adds a sloped appearance to any shoulder, so if you already have a strong slope, this only highlights it.

• **Wide necklines:** These can fall off your shoulders and won't flatter your neckline.

• **Wide straps:** Straps that are set far apart from each other most likely fall out of place, leaving you constantly pulling and tugging at your straps. Who needs all that extra work?

SHOULDER WORKOUT

Many of us live in front of our computers. While working in the information age has vastly improved our knowledge, it certainly hasn't helped our posture. Everywhere we look we see people hunched over their desks with sloped shoulders, their heads pushed forward to see the screen, and their backs rounded. Usually, these are the clients who come to us saying they have flab around their bra strap areas and that no matter what they do they can't get their triceps, biceps, or back toned. Sound familiar?

It doesn't have to be that way. To restore your body to its anatomically correct position—and to develop smashingly toned shoulders—do our recommended moves (or just toss your laptop). By working your shoulders and front, side, and rear deltoids, you'll feel stronger, have less upper-back pain, and look more confident.

You'll need:

- Dumbbells
- A bench

How much weight should you use? Use dumbbells between 2 and 5 pounds.

Training Guidelines

1. Do all of the following nine moves in the order provided. The first five moves make up the shoulder series:
   - Athletic stance serving trays
   - Lateral raises
   - Barbie (doll) arms
   - Touchdown goalposts
   - Flat-back rear delt
   - Plank hold
   - Step-up with alternating shoulder press
   - Squat 'n' swing
   - Shoulder cross 'n' squat
2. Repeat the entire sequence two to three times, back-to-back.
3. Do this workout two to three times a week.

ASHLEY'S TIP: Do the abs series first to warm up your core. (See Chapter 5.)

The Moves

These shoulder moves will really make a difference in your overall physique.

Athletic Stance Serving Trays -------------------------

This rotator cuff exercise helps your shoulder-to-arm connection look even stronger (Figure 3.4).

1. Start in athletic stance, and set your spine. Holding a dumbbell in each hand, position both arms at 90-degree angles at your sides, palms facing in, as if you were holding a clutch purse under each arm.
2. Open your arms out to the sides so your palms are parallel with your body. Push your shoulders down and your elbows slightly forward.
3. Return to neutral position, and repeat 10 times, keeping your spine aligned.

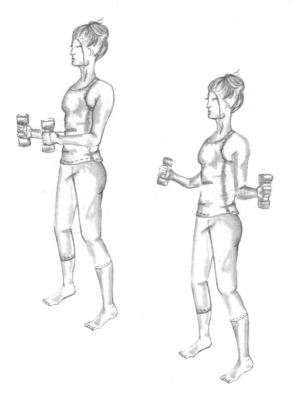

Figure 3.4.
Athletic stance
serving trays.

Lateral Raises ---

1. Start in athletic stance, and set your spine. Hold a dumbbell in each hand with your arms at your sides, palms facing your thighs (Figure 3.5).

Figure 3.5. Lateral raises. Keep your shoulders pressing away from your ears.

2. Slowly raise your arms out to the sides to shoulder height and try to separate your shoulder blades. Lower your arms down to starting position, and repeat 10 times.

ASHLEY'S TIP: Keep your shoulders pressing away from your ears at all times. Keep your wrists strong and tight as you hold and lift the weight.

Barbie (Doll) Arms ---------------------------------------

1. Start in athletic stance, and set your spine. Hold a dumbbell in
   each hand with your arms extended at the front
   of your thighs, palms facing each other.

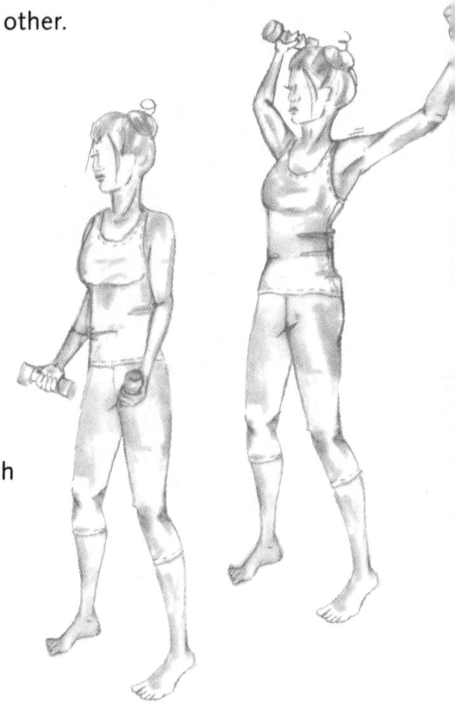

*Figure 3.6.
Barbie (doll)
arms. Raise
your arms
back like
Barbie would!*

2. Tilt the weights at an angle
   so that your thumbs face up
   and your pinkies point down. Push
   your shoulders down away from
   your ears, slightly bending your
   elbows, and inhale.
3. Bring both arms up, arcing them
   over your head to face the back
   wall as if you were rotating the
   arms of a Barbie doll (Figure
   3.6). Return to starting position,
   and repeat 10 times.

Touchdown Goalposts ==================================

1. Start in athletic stance, and set your spine. Holding a dumbbell in
   each hand, press down your shoulder blades.
2. Bring both elbows out to the side with your forearms at 90-degree
   angles, palms facing inward.
3. Leading with your thumb (but not rotating your wrist), rotate your
   forearms toward the back wall as if you're making a goalpost sign
   with your arms (Figure 3.7). Repeat 10 times.

ASHLEY'S TIP:  To make this more advanced, stand on one leg, alternating legs halfway through the set.

Figure 3.7.
Touchdown goalposts. Bring
your arms up to say, "Score!"

Flat-Back Rear Delt -

1. Start in athletic stance, and set your spine. Hold dumbbells at your sides and push your shoulders away from your ears.
2. Bend your torso forward at the waist so your back is parallel to the ground. Keep your eyes focused on the floor, arms reaching straight down to the ground with your palms facing the back wall.
3. Extend your arms directly out in line with your shoulders as if you were an airplane (Figure 3.8). Both arms should reach for opposite walls as if you're pulling your shoulder blades apart. Bring your arms down, and repeat 10 times.

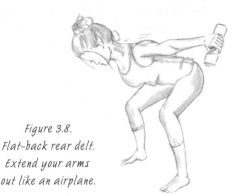

Figure 3.8.
Flat-back rear delt.
Extend your arms
out like an airplane.

ASHLEY'S TIP: Keep your shoulders pressing away from your ears at all times. To make this more advanced, try it on one leg. Shift your weight to one leg, and fire, or contract, the glute of the standing leg. Then push the opposite leg straight back with your foot flexed in the air. Repeat each side 5 times.

Plank Hold -

1. Start at the top of a raised push-up position, keeping your feet shoulder-width apart (Figure 3.9). Squeeze your glutes, and pull your belly button in. Spread your fingers wide, keeping pressure between the thumb and index finger.
2. Press away from the floor as if you were trying to keep the floor from rising up. Hold this position for 20 seconds. Inhale for 4 counts; then exhale for 8 counts.
3. Keep your belly button pulled in toward your spine, and lower your knees to the floor. Rest for 10 seconds. Repeat 5 times.

Figure 3.9.
Plank hold. Don't let your
hips sag like a camel!

ASHLEY'S TIP: Don't let your hips sag toward the floor like a camel. To make this more challenging, try balancing on only one arm while maintaining the plank position, alternating each side 4 times.

Step-Up with Alternating Shoulder Press ---------------

1. Stand behind a sturdy bench, holding a dumbbell in each hand. Bend your elbows with your hands raised next to your shoulders, palms facing inward (Figure 3.10).
2. Step your left foot onto the bench, and push through your left heel. Squeeze your glutes, and keep your abs pulled in. As you step up with your left foot, bring your right knee up to waist height with a flexed foot.
3. At the top, push your left arm up and overhead, pushing it slightly behind your ears. Simultaneously, lower your right arm down by your side, pushing it slightly behind your torso.
4. Carefully step down, leading with your right foot, and bring your arms back to starting position. Repeat 10 times. Switch legs, and repeat another 10 times.

Figure 3.10. Step up with the alternating shoulder press.

Squat 'n' Swing

1. Start in athletic stance, and set your spine. Holding dumbbells at your sides, squat back and down like you're sitting in a chair, your back straight and tilted forward in line with your head (Figure 3.11).
2. As you press back up to athletic stance, push one arm back up to "Barbie arm" position (like the stiff arms of a Barbie doll), slightly behind your head.
3. Press your opposite arm back through the triceps with your glutes fired and your belly pulled in. Each time you squat, alternate arms. Repeat 10 times with both arms.

ASHLEY'S TIP: To make this more challenging, try balancing on one leg as you stand up from the squat.

Figure 3.11.
Squat 'n' swing.
Step up and raise
one Barbie arm.

Shoulder Cross 'n' Squat ----------------------------------

1. Start in athletic stance, and set your spine. Hold a dumbbell in your right hand.
2. As you slowly bend your knees to squat as if sitting in a chair, bring your right hand across your body so your wrist is touching your left knee (Figure 3.12). Both elbows should be slightly bent with your shoulders pressing back and down.
3. As you press up back to starting position, press your right arm up and back with your palm facing forward and your wrist and elbow in a straight line, as if you're the Statue of Liberty. Your arm should be slightly behind your ear. Repeat 5 times.
4. Put the dumbbell in your left hand, and repeat another 5 times.

ASHLEY'S TIP: For a more advanced move, lift your left leg up as you cross to the left. As you cross to the right, bring your right leg up.

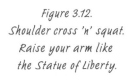

Figure 3.12.
Shoulder cross 'n' squat.
Raise your arm like
the Statue of Liberty.

FRAMING YOURSELF

Having strong shoulders helps you function, lift, and move. It also gives your whole physique a nice shape. Just think of shoulder toning as adding a picture frame around a gorgeous piece of art. Without the frame, the painting is still impressive, but once the frame is added, it's a masterpiece. Wearing the right clothes, just like adding the right lighting for the art, just enhances the effect even more.

Now that you've worked out your shoulders and they are toned and gorgeous, get ready to strengthen your back.

Bringing Sexy Back

4

Strengthen and Accentuate Your Other Side

We tend to ignore our back. We don't pay much attention to it when we shop for new clothes or get dressed in the morning, not even when we're at the gym. But the back is one of the prettiest parts of the body. And backs aren't just pretty—they're *sexy*. Even showing a little cleavage seems more conservative than donning an open-back top. Everything from our necks down to our butts affects how our back looks, so accentuating the back involves dressing right for our neck, bust, and waist, too. Using our training and fashion techniques can take your back off the back burner and give it the attention it deserves.

Back Tips

Let's start with the neck and work our way down.

If you think you have a long neck, *do* wear:

- **Turtlenecks:** These look amazing on you! Turtlenecks and mock turtlenecks, short sleeve and sleeveless all work with your long neck.

- **Funnel necks:** Funnel necks are similar to turtlenecks but only come two-thirds of the way up your neck and don't fold over.

PAIGE SAYS: A funnel neck is a neckline that comes up higher than a mock turtleneck and lower than a turtleneck. It hits at the Adam's apple or throat and sits upward in the shape of an inverted funnel. A mock turtleneck clings tightly to the lower neck.

• **Blouses:** Try wearing a blouse with the top two buttons open, highlighting your lovely neck and chest.

PAIGE'S TIP: Bold necklaces, dangly earrings, and sensational chokers can be your best friends; experiment and enjoy. Scarves tied around your neck also look fabulous.

If you think you have a long neck, *don't* wear:

• **Deep-U or strapless tops:** If your neck is particularly long, these might not be your best bets. Front or back, you've already got plenty to show with your long, lovely neck, so there's no need to show even more skin above your bustline.

If you have a short neck, *do* wear:

• **Deep-U tops or V-necks:** These necklines elongate the neck and chest region as well as your back.

• **Off-the-shoulder tops:** The lower neckline elongates your shorter neck.

• **Strapless dresses:** These can have a great camouflage effect as they draw the eye down away from your neck (Figure 4.1). Because this style exposes the neck, shoulder, and chest area simultaneously, it suggests a longer, leaner neck.

If you have a short neck, *don't* wear:

• **Turtlenecks, mock turtlenecks, and funnel necks:** Fabric around your neck just attracts attention to your neck's shorter length. If you live in a colder climate where turtlenecks are a necessity, opt for a thinner fabric that won't bulk around the neck, or choose a more swooping cowl neckline.

Figure 4.1.
Do go strapless.

PAIGE'S TIP: ⤵ How you accessorize really matters. Long, dangly earrings make your neck seem more compact. Avoid these and opt for dazzling studs or smaller settings. The same goes for chokers. Pick a delicate necklace with a longer length or a cascading piece instead.

Under Armor

So you're wearing the perfect outfit for your body type, you're toting a hot new purse, your stilettos look fabulous, and you're out the door on the way to a promising date. Then you happen to glance behind you in the bathroom mirror—oh no! There it is. The tight lines of your bra peeking out from under your perfect new top, with flesh bulging over. What now? Well, grab a wrap, get going, and enjoy yourself—you have more important things to think about!

But tomorrow head to your favorite lingerie shop and get yourself fitted for the right size bra. If your bra is leaving a mark around your sides, maybe it's time to rethink your high school bra size. Go for a larger number. The cup size (the letter) could still be fine. When trying on bras, make sure they fit comfortably on the middle hook. If you're struggling to close a bra on the loosest hook, go up another size. No matter what the number is, it's better to wear clothes that fit.

Even if you've been the same size your whole life, never buy a new bra without trying it on, especially a lace bra. There's a big difference between scratchy and comfy lace—try it on before enduring a day of misery in an itchy bra.

A few musts for your lingerie drawer:

- A thin-strapped bra (nude and black)
- A thick-strapped bra (nude and black)
- A racerback bra (nude and black)
- A strapless bra (nude and black)
- A colorful print or lacey bra
- A seamless T-shirt bra
- A push-up bra

GENTLE CYCLE

*A*ll the wear-and-tear from washing your bras can stretch them out or shrink them. To preserve your bras for as long as possible, wash them in a lingerie bag on the gentle cycle and tumble dry low. Just as with jeans, if you apply too much heat on your bras, you'll blow out the Lycra and lose the elasticity, and the bras will start riding up your back. Wash them in warm, not hot, water and hang them to dry.

Back to Back

There are two main back shapes: *flat* and *rounded.* You can tell which one you have by standing against a wall. If your entire back is flush against it and doesn't bow out in the middle or lower back, you have a flat back. Having a flat back looks similar to someone wearing a back brace: you're completely vertical.

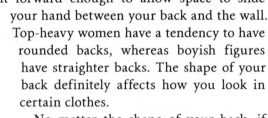

A rounded back means you have a slight protrusion in your shoulders. By no means are you the Hunchback of Notre Dame, but your shoulders tilt forward enough to allow space to slide your hand between your back and the wall. Top-heavy women have a tendency to have rounded backs, whereas boyish figures have straighter backs. The shape of your back definitely affects how you look in certain clothes.

No matter the shape of your back, if you feel yours is a little fleshy or you tend to carry weight in your back, try not to wear anything too restrictive, including tight bras. Opt for softer fabrications, empire-waist tops, drapey fabrics, and button-downs with softer silhouettes. You might feel more comfortable passing on the tighter Lycra tops or open-back styles.

Figure 4.2. These keyhole openings in the back work to flatter backs.

If you have a flat back, *do* wear:

- **Keyhole openings:** Look for tops with these flattering openings in the back (Figure 4.2). They are your key to looking fantastic, giving you the illusion of having more curves.

> **PAIGE'S TIP:** Tank tops with a keyhole opening toward the bottom of your back can give you more shape where you want it and add a point of interest to an ill-defined area. A keyhole opening can be in the front or back of a garment and has an oval shape that is narrow in width and long in length. Front keyhole openings usually start at the neckline and plunge downward to show off cleavage.

- **Shirts that drape or cowl in the back:** These show off that gorgeous back of yours by adding depth and definition.

- **Low-back halter tops:** These kinds of halters dip low in the back in a V- or U-shape, giving the appearance of curvature at the small of your back.

If you have a flat back, *don't* wear:

- **Strapless tops or dresses:** It might be harder for them to stay up where you want them if your back is flat and curveless.

If you have a rounded back, *do* wear:

- **Strapless tops or dresses:** To make the strapless dress look even better on you, pair it with a necklace or scarf that hangs down your back.

- **Halter dresses:** Find a dress where the back hits above your waistline (Figure 4.3).

- **Thicker straps:** Look for tank tops with thicker straps, because they'll disguise your rounded back and shoulders.

- **Shawls:** Make use of these soft and sexy accessories to adorn and cover up.

Figure 4.3.
Low-back halters create curves.

PAIGE'S TIP: 🎒 Carry a lightweight messenger bag, and switch it from shoulder to shoulder every couple of hours to avoid the shoulder slump.

If you have a rounded back, *don't* wear:

• **Off-the-shoulder tops:** These only highlight the rounded shape of your back.

Waisting Away

Knowing whether you are short- or long-waisted is critical for dressing right for your body type. To find out your waist type, follow these two steps.

1. Take the following measurements:
   • Leg length: Measure from the top of your hip bone to the floor.
   • Center back: Measure from the top of your spine (i.e., the larger protruding bone you feel just below the base of your neck) to your natural waist. Your natural waist is where your waist naturally curves inward. This is about an inch above your belly button.
2. Divide your leg length by your center back measurement. For example, if your center back is 14 inches and your leg length is 34 inches, then divide 34 by 14, which equals 2.4.

You are long-waisted and shorter-legged if the result is *less* than 2.7. You are short-waisted and longer-legged if the result is *more* than 2.7. In the preceding example, you would be long-waisted and shorter-legged.

If you're short-waisted, *do* wear:

• **A top or dress that falls slightly off your shoulders:** Look for a top that has a slight V-shape in the back to elongate your torso.

• **Drop-waisted dresses or shirts:** Ideal for lengthening the torso, these make you look even longer and leaner.

• **Blouson or princess tops and empire waists:** These styles are great to help even out your proportions.

PAIGE SAYS: A blouson is a type of dress, jacket, or tunic that usually has a dropped waistline seam, where the fabric drapes and is tightly banded at the bottom (Figure 4.4).

- **Tunics:** These longer tops lengthen your midsection (Figure 4.5).

- **Tops that drape in the back:** Make sure they fall past your waistline to accentuate your figure.

- **Low-rise jeans:** Look for low-rise jeans to lengthen your torso. Finding a pair with a wider waistband helps create the illusion of having a dropped waist.

Figure 4.4.
Blouson tops even
out proportions.

PAIGE SAYS: *Low-rise* describes pants and skirts that hit below the natural waistline. A low rise occurs when a garment's total front rise is about seven and a half inches or less.

If you're short-waisted, *don't* wear:

- **High-rise pants or skirts:** The higher waist draws attention to your shorter torso.

PAIGE SAYS: *High-rise* describes any garment with a waistline that sits higher than your natural waistline. However, when it comes to jeans, a high rise can be anything with a total front rise of nine inches or more.

- **High-rise jeans:** Anything that cuts your midsection in half evenly also shortens it.

- **Crop tops:** Opt for tops that are longer and lengthen your look.

- **Wide belts:** These just accentuate the placement of your middle. Instead, wear

Figure 4.5.
Tunics lengthen
your middle.

Figure 4.6.
A bolero jacket doesn't look great on short-waisted women.

a narrow belt around your waist in the same color as the top you're wearing. Or try slinging a belt around your hips to fake a lower waistline.

- **Bolero jackets:** Avoid jackets that are cropped right at your waist (Figure 4.6). These jackets or coats hit above the waistline. The name of these jackets originates from a dance called the bolero.

If you're long-waisted, *do* wear:

- **Tops that drape or cowl in the back:** These stunners flatter your figure, but they should end at or slightly above your waist for maximum "wow" factor.

- **Strapless tops and dresses:** Go for straighter lines, and find tops that come up right below your shoulder blades.

- **Blazers:** Jackets that hit slightly below the waist are your best bet for outerwear.

- **Long blouses:** Don't tuck them in, and to elongate your body pick shirts in softer fabrics such as silks, chiffons, and satins.

- **A-line dresses:** These are always flattering and look wonderful with your figure.

- **High-rise jeans:** Look for jeans that hit just below your belly button or at your waist.

> **PAIGE SAYS:** Butt cleavage, the separation between the top of a person's butt cheeks, is usually accentuated by pants, skirts, or jeans that are too low on the backside.

If you're long-waisted, *don't* wear:

- **Belts that match your top:** Instead, pick belts in a different color to create space separation on your lithe upper body.

- **Low-rise jeans:** The low waist will make your torso look even longer.

HOW DO YOU KNOW IF YOUR JEANS ARE TOO LOW?

*D*o the "sit-down test" in the dressing room. If you sit with your back to the mirror (if there's no chair, just do a squat) and show any butt cleavage (or "plumber's crack"), take those lovelies off. Stay away from jeans that show any extra skin unless you're planning on only standing in them. If you're buying the jeans just to go dancing or walk down the runway, which is not likely for most of us, then feel free to grab them—but remember not to sit down. For all-purpose jeans, find a pair with a more-fitting waistline that won't expose your nether regions.

WE GOT YOUR BACK

A lot of us have "mirror body syndrome": we work out only the parts of our bodies that we can see in the mirror. We tend to neglect strengthening our backs—until we realize we have to wear an open-back dress and we start to panic. But having a strong back is critically important for everyday functioning, not just for how we look in clothes. Most of our day-to-day activities require us to bend forward: we lift groceries, we pick up our kids, we sit at computers, we sketch, and we cook. When we reach forward that much, we need to strengthen our opposite muscles (i.e., our back muscles). Keeping the back strong and flexible is imperative for preventing injuries: we're always rotating our backs into different positions, and we need to be able to move and stay flexible.

The back consists of several different muscle groups: lats, rhomboids, spinal erectors, and rear deltoids. The top, middle, and lower back can all be strengthened with different exercises. But working out *all* parts of the back is essential for standing up straight and using your body most efficiently.

It's time to make your back strong and sexy.

You'll need:

- Dumbbells (between 2 and 5 pounds)
- A medium-resistance band

How much weight should you use? If you can't clear 10 reps with a certain weight, it's too heavy. Go down in weight.

Training Guidelines

1. Do all five moves below in any order you like. For example:
   - Close grip rows
   - Supermans
   - Lat pulldowns
   - Flat-back reverse fly
   - Cat and dog
2. Repeat the series two to three times, back-to-back.
3. Do this workout (with the moves in any order) two to three times a week.

ASHLEY'S TIP: Do the shoulders series first to warm up your upper body. (See Chapter 3.)

The Moves

The back will look stunning once you start following these exercises.

Supermans -

1. Start on all fours with your hands in line with your shoulders. Keep your head in line with your spine and your knees in line with your hip bones. Curl your toes under, and look down. Pull your belly button in.
2. Without letting the middle of your back sink down, extend your right arm out in front

of you with your thumb facing up while simultaneously pushing your left leg straight back (Figure 4.7).

3. Flex your back foot, and push through your heel. Fire (contract) your glute. Hold for 5 seconds. Return to starting position on all fours.

4. Repeat 5 times. Then repeat 5 times with the opposite hand and foot (your left arm and your right leg).

ASHLEY'S TIP: Don't let your body shift from side to side when you're extending out. Make sure you're pulling your belly in and not dropping your back. To make this more challenging, strap 2-pound weights to your wrists and ankles.

Figure 4.7.
Extend the body for
Supermans.

Lat Pulldowns

ASHLEY'S TIP: If you have a large bust, it's particularly important to work your lats to balance out your physique.

1. Loop a medium-resistance band over a pull-up bar. Kneel on your knees with your tush lifted off your heels, and curl your toes under, making sure your torso is straight up and down. Keep your glutes tight and your belly in.

2. Hold a handle of the band in each hand with your palms facing inward. Block your shoulders down toward your waist (Figure 4.8).

ASHLEY SAYS: To block your shoulders down means sliding both shoulder blades away from your ears before you start an exercise.

3. Pull both elbows straight down toward your waist, keeping your chest lifted. Bring them back to the starting position, and repeat 15 times.

Figure 4.8.
Block your shoulders down
when doing lat pulldowns.

ASHLEY'S TIP: You should *not* feel this exercise in your
neck. Don't push your shoulders forward; keep your head in line
with your spine.

Close Grip Rows

1. Sit on the ground with your back straight, shoulders down, knees
   bent, heels on the ground, and toes flexed up. Take a medium-

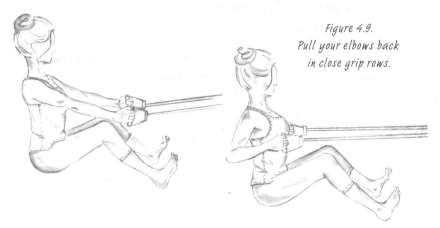

Figure 4.9.
Pull your elbows back
in close grip rows.

resistance band, and loop it around a stable surface at chest height, such as a table leg.

2. Hold the handles of the band with your palms facing in. Extend your arms straight with tension on the band. Avoid the death grip. Block your shoulders down.

3. Pull your elbows straight back, wrapping them around your back as if you were squeezing a small tree between your shoulder blades (Figure 4.9). Don't push your shoulders forward when pulling the band back. Return to your starting position, and repeat 15 times.

Flat-Back Reverse Fly -----------------------

1. Start in athletic stance (or sit on floor), and set your spine. Push your shoulders down away from your ears, holding dumbbells at your sides.

2. Bend your torso forward at your waist so your back is parallel to the ground, your eyes looking at the floor. Let your arms hang down to the floor with your elbows slightly bent, palms facing each other.

3. Leading with your elbows—not your hands—bring both elbows up and back behind you, squeezing your shoulder blades back and down as if you're crushing a softball between them (Figure 4.10). Avoid the death grip.

4. Squeeze and hold. Bring your elbows back down to the starting position and repeat 10 times.

Figure 4.10.
Lead with your elbows in flat-back reverse flys.

Cat and Dog --

1. Start on all fours with your hands in line with your shoulders. Keep your head in line with your spine and your knees in line with your hip bones. Curl your toes under, and look down. Pull your belly button in.
2. Exhale and tuck your chin to your throat, and tuck your pelvis under (arching your spine like a cat). Hold. Squeeze your glutes.
3. Inhale. Extend your spine with your chest reaching to the wall in front of you. Rotate your tailbone up to the ceiling, and pull your shoulders back (Figure 4.11). Hold. Repeat 10 times.

Figure 4.11.
Find your inner animal when doing the cat and dog.

BACK WORDS

Don't neglect the parts of your body that you can't see, and remember to include this workout as part of your weekly rotation. Training your back helps reduce back and neck pain, improves your posture (making you appear more confident), and gives you the strength to carry the weight of the world on your shoulders . . . with proper form!

Abs-solutely Perfect

5

The Tummy You Always Wanted

In today's crazy world, it's more important than ever to stay centered. There's no better way to do that than to focus on our own center: our core.

Our abdominal muscles are at the very core of our being. All that we consume gets processed through our stomachs to nourish our bodies. We breathe deeply through our diaphragms and lungs. We create human life through our reproductive system and carry children in our wombs. Our abdominal walls serve as a protective shield surrounding all of our vital organs. It's no wonder that in Eastern philosophy, the center of our energy (our chi), which emanates from the core, is so cherished. In the West, the core is known as our trunk, our powerhouse, and our internal girdle. When you focus on your abs, you're truly improving your body from the inside out.

But don't get us wrong: the abs aren't too sacred to whip into shape! We still want your midsection to look as rockin' as possible. Through our fashion and fitness tips, we'll help you look fabulous down to your very core.

DRESSING FASHION-AB-LY

Finding the right outfits to "trick the eye" or flaunt your abs can be a cinch if you follow our tips:

If your stomach's not as flat as you'd like it to be, *do* wear:

● **Dark colors on top:** Dark colors tend to show less shape and texture variation, which helps mask those little belly bulges.

● **Silky or chiffon blouses:** These flowy fabrics lie softly against the body giving the midsection a nice smooth shape. Nothing makes you feel more feminine than silk or chiffon.

*Figure 5.1.
Banded bottoms help
disguise extra folds.*

● **Tops with banded bottoms:** Sweatshirt-style tops that are loose on top but have a banded bottom are a great way to hide those pesky extra folds (Figure 5.1).

● **Trousers with sewn-down pleats or a flat front:** Flat pleats can offer a girdle effect and flatten out your tummy.

● **Blouson tops:** This style, which has lots of extra fabric in the stomach region, not only masks the tummy but is incredibly comfortable too!

● **Loose sweaters:** Cozy and delicious, these staples disguise your upper body under a blanket of warmth. Try to find sweaters with a bit of shape, and avoid a boxy, cropped number; this only makes your upper half look wide and shapeless.

● **A-line skirts:** This style does the trick by drawing focus to the shape of the skirt and not to your midsection, but make sure that the skirt isn't too tight (Figure 5.2).

● **Drop-waist designs:** The lower waist draws the eye down and bypasses the belly.

● **Tops that hit your hipline:** Longer tops create a longer silhouette, which has an undeniably slimming effect.

● **Full-length coats:** For maximum waist-enhancing effect, try a trench style with a belted waist (Figure 5.3).

● **Double-waistband jeans:** Jeans with a thicker waistband and a double button hold you in where you need it most. Make sure the wide waistband hits at the biggest part of your stomach.

● **Leggings or skinny pants with a tunic-style top:** The longer top paired with the slender bottoms gives you a long, lean look.

Figure 5.2.
This A-line skirt is just right for your abs.

● **Button-down shirts:** As long as they're not too boxy, these tailored classics can give you a clean shape and a put-together look.

● **Wide V-neck necklines and big collars:** These necklines draw attention away from your middle and focus on your fabulous shoulders and sexy collarbone.

● **Puffed sleeves:** These delicate sleeves enhance your arms and create a clever diversion away from your abdominal area. These sleeves can also make the waist look smaller by adding some width to the shoulders.

If your stomach's not as flat as you'd like it to be, *don't* wear:

● **Anything too clingy:** Enough said.

● **Bolero jackets:** These cropped jackets hit at just the wrong place. Opt for longer blazers to enhance your physique.

● **Narrow, fitted skirts:** The straight cut of this skirt can accentuate any fullness you might have in your midsection.

Figure 5.3.
Trench coats accentuate a smaller waist.

A-line skirts are a better alternative because they widen at the bottom, making your waist look smaller.

- **Crop tops:** These are pretty much always a no-no. Even if your abs are fab, these still belong only in the gym or back in the 1980s.

- **Full skirts:** Too much gathering or pleating at the top of the skirt can make your middle look fuller.

- **Double-breasted jackets:** The square-shaped arrangement of the buttons on this type of blazer can widen your midsection. Stick to single-breasted blazers for a more slimming look.

- **Low-rise jeans or jeans that are very high-waisted:** The low waist lets it all hang out, while the high waist leads to a poochy middle. Stick to medium-waisted, classic-rise jeans for the best fit. These jeans fall below the belly button, but above the hip bone.

- **Skinny or superwide belts:** Cutting your stomach in half might not give you the look you want. Try belting below the waist at the hips.

- **Horizontal stripes:** These just accentuate the circumference of your midriff.

- **Full or bell sleeves:** Wearing a top with long sleeves that significantly bell out can actually make your middle look fuller, especially when you stand with your arms at your sides. Look for a sleeve with a straight or fitted shape.

- **Muumuus:** You never need this much fabric from head to toe. You can still have oodles of style while camouflaging your middle. Try a babydoll or empire-waist dress for a little added shape.

- **Large purses:** Try not to carry large handbags that hit right at your waist. Opt for smaller purses or totes.

- **Scarves:** Don't think you're fooling anyone by tying printed scarves or sweaters around your hips. Tie them around your shoulders for a lengthening look.

Undergarment Patrol

The key to slenderizing your middle is wearing the right under-garments. Lingerie that holds you in—even control-top panty-hose—can still look beautiful and sexy. Buy lingerie in the styles and colors you like, and let it do its job.

If you're uncomfortable with your tummy, *do* wear:

• **Babydoll negligees:** Babydoll nighties are sexy, flirty, and fun (Figure 5.4). These little gowns with empire seams under the bust hit mid-thigh and drape softly over the body. Select from a variety of fun prints and fabrics—these darlings are flattering on all body types.

• **Chemises:** If you're uncomfortable show-ing a lot of leg but still love the babydoll style, opt for a chemise. This A-line, thin-strapped, loosely fitted nightgown or negligee that gently skims the body can be belted and is highly forgiving in nature. It hits beautifully below the knees and has that air of old-school Hollywood glamour. The best chemises cover your tummy, hips, and thighs in a soft, drapey fabric, such as stretch silk or satin, and are über-romantic.

• **High-rise boy shorts:** Find boy shorts that hit just below the belly button in a thicker, substantial fabric such as Lycra. Try not to get super-high-waist boy shorts, or they'll look like grandma pant-ies! They should be cut high enough up on your leg to show just a little butt cheek. These are particularly great if you have a great butt and legs, since these shorts draw attention away from your tummy and toward your other assets. Fun prints and stripes can be playful.

Figure 5.4.
These babydoll nighties are flirty and fun.

• **Loose camisole tops with matching panties:** These silky, satin pieces can be worn in and out of the bedroom. Make sure the top slightly skims the body in a looser fabric.

• **Bustier-style bras:** These structured bras with metal and wire boning look insanely good under blazers or just hidden beneath clothes (Figure 5.5). Keep the bustier long enough so it doesn't cut off right in the middle of your tummy. Do a sit-down test—if the bustier cuts into your middle, find a longer one.

Figure 5.5.
Bustier tops look
great under blazers!

• **Tank tops with built-in bras:** Soft cotton, modal Lycra tanks with built-in bras are fabulous for wearing in and out of the bedroom; they cover your tummy, and they look great underneath sheer blouses.

• **Classic wrap robe:** Everyone can use a comfy robe to start the day. The thinner the fabric, the more flattering it is on your belly. Look for wider waist ties to make your tummy seem more petite. Avoid robes that are too fuzzy, furry, or thick, unless you don't mind drawing a little attention to your middle.

• **Miniskirt slips:** These aren't your grandmother's slips! Lycra miniskirt slips act as a girdle by holding in your belly with thicker fabric. The heavier fabric prevents them from riding up and creating too much static cling.

• **Leggings:** Wearing spandex leggings under a miniskirt or dress can hold you in and help smooth out your middle.

If you feel great about your abs, *do* wear:

• **Low-rise boy shorts:** The lower waist shows off your stomach while accentuating your butt and thighs.

• **Tight camisole tops:** Fitted Lycra or thin cotton camisoles look great on you and show off your toned tummy.

- **Classic robes:** Robes with thin waistbands in thin fabrics will show off your taut middle.

Also, babydolls, bustier tops, and nightgowns in tight fabrics at any length work great on you, too!

Beach Bonanza

For many people, finding the right swimsuit is sheer torture. Who looks good half-naked under bright dressing-room lights? Internet shopping has never seemed more appealing. Never fear! Shopping for swimwear can be much more efficient and enjoyable if you know what styles flatter your body the most.

If you're really proud of your abs, *do* wear:

- **Low-rise string bikinis:** Go for it!

If you think your tummy is a little poochy, *do* wear:

- **Low-rise bikini bottoms with bust-enhancing bikini tops:** The more you enhance your bust, the smaller your waist will seem.

PAIGE'S TIP: Try to avoid bikinis that don't have enough bust support. Look for underwire support if you have larger breasts. Triangular tops are better for those of you with smaller breasts. Sagging breasts just draw more attention to your middle. Also, your bikini top and bottom don't have to be identical. Wearing a solid color on the bottom with a print on the top focuses the eye upward and away from your belly.

- **One-piece bathing suits:** One-piece suits can look smashing and are a great way to mask a belly. Pair a one-piece with a matching wraparound, A-line flare miniskirt to give you more shape. If you think you have a thicker waist, look for a one-piece with vertical stripes on the top and bottom and a solid color around your middle. It looks like you're wearing a cinched-in belt. The darker color in the middle gives you more of an hourglass effect.

- **Tankinis:** Tank-top-style bikini tops that extend down to your bikini bottoms are great in a nice, thick Lycra or spandex material. The tighter fabric holds in your stomach and tends to stay put when swimming. These are a stylish, sexy alternative to a one-piece swimsuit. Plus, the tank can play double duty as a top.

- **Blouson swimsuits:** A blouson swim top is like a tankini but isn't fitted on top—it blouses out on the top and ties on the side at your hip bone (Figure 5.6). A print on top with a solid color on the bottom distracts from your belly. Stick with contemporary prints and styles so you don't look like you've borrowed your grandmother's suit.

- **One-piece swimsuits with mesh in the middle:** The band of mesh across the middle of this swimsuit gives the illusion of a bikini while still camouflaging the belly.

- **Wraps:** Have fun with these island-inspired accessories. They come in so many styles from a sheer tunic to a cotton wraparound cloth skirt and are fabulous for hiding tummy trouble. They can also double as a fun and fresh skirt!

- **Board shorts:** Cute board shorts (fitted short bottoms that lace up in the front) look good with any kind of style on top, particularly halters. High-waisted shorts that have an upward leg opening brings the eye upward instead of cutting across your leg.

Figure 5.6.
Find fresh colors to keep the blouson suit looking young.

CORE BELIEFS

Working your abs means strengthening your core muscle group. The core is what people refer to as the girdle of your waistline that wraps around and supports the rest of your body. It includes your abs, lower abs, and lower back. It's your "tree" of stability for all the other movements in life. When you have a strong core and know how to engage it properly, you have more functional strength for daily-life tasks, making you less prone to injury.

It's also important to find and then strengthen your pelvic floor (your pelvic muscles). How do you know if you have a weak pelvic floor? Here's a laywoman's test: if you pee when you laugh, exercise, or cough, chances are your pelvic muscles are weak. If you've had a baby, you're more likely to have a weaker pelvic floor. The wonderful news is that just about anyone can strengthen and connect to her pelvic floor and the rest of her core. Taking the time to focus on and execute the following core exercises will change the way you move through life and result in a flatter tummy!

Most people are convinced that there's one magic pill, exercise machine, or food plan that will give them six-pack abs. We hate to be the bearers of bad news, but it's not true. Rather, it takes a consistent combination of the proper food, adequate water intake, cardio exercise, and training. You can do abs exercises until the cows come home, but to see your abdominal wall, you need to melt away the body fat first.

Bloating also makes it harder to see results in your abs. High-sodium foods (e.g., smoked meats, salty snack foods, canned foods, and soy sauce), dairy, things in husks (e.g., corn, popcorn, brown rice), and soda lead to bloating and can make you look heavier than you really are. Mental note: don't scarf down a huge tub of popcorn before a night out on the town if you want flat abs.

Another misconception about abs exercises is that you have to feel the burn to know the moves are working. For some variations, such as floor Kegel exercises, you squeeze your "pee-flow" muscle, which results in a slight cramping sensation rather than a typical burn—but that's what you're supposed to feel. The key to remember is not to push out against your ab wall, but to pull your abs in toward your spine to avoid a distended tummy. If you feel like you're pushing in a similar manner to when you're going to the bathroom (sorry to be crass!), then you're not working your core in the right way.

ASHLEY SAYS: The pee-flow muscle is the muscle you use to stop the flow of urine; it is more commonly called the pelvic muscle.

You'll need:

- A properly sized stability ball; if you're 5 feet to 5 feet 6 inches tall, use a 55-centimeter ball; if you're 5 feet 7 inches or taller, use a 65-centimeter ball
- A yoga or gym mat

Training Guidelines

1. Do all the following six moves in any order you like. For example:
   - Karate punch and twist
   - Roll 'em and shoot 'em
   - Hairwash
   - Half toothpaste roll
   - Side planks
   - Waist whittler
2. Repeat the sequence two to three times, back-to-back.
3. Do this workout (with the moves in any order) three to four times a week.

   ASHLEY'S TIP: Do individual abs moves in conjunction with other body-part workouts, interspersing one abs move between sets; connecting with your core helps improve the form and effectiveness of any workout.

The Moves

Repeat these abs moves to strengthen your core.

   ASHLEY'S TIP: If you have forward-sloping shoulders, place a small folded-up towel underneath the small protruding bone on the lower half of your skull, your occipital bone, when you're doing floor exercises. This helps even out your alignment.

Half Toothpaste Roll ----------------------------------

1. Lie down as if you're about to do a sit-up; interlace hands behind your head, and bring both shoulder blades off the ground (Figure 5.7). Keep your eyes on your chest, and inhale deeply.

Figure 5.7.
Curl up like a tube
of toothpaste in the
half toothpaste roll.

2. As you exhale, draw your pelvic floor in toward your belly button. Tuck the pubic bones in toward the belly button. Squeeze your glutes. Hold.
3. Roll down one vertebra at a time. Repeat 5 times.

Roll 'Em and Shoot 'Em

1. Lie down on your back, reaching behind your ears to hold onto the legs of a weight bench, a sturdy ottoman, or a friend's ankles. Pull your knees in toward your belly button with your legs at a 90-degree angle and your feet flexed.
2. Inhale and roll your spine back toward your face like a baby having its diaper changed (Figure 5.8).

3. Slowly exhale and unroll your spine one vertebra at a time until it's completely flat on the floor. As your spine hits the ground, pull one knee in toward your neck with your foot flexed and the other knee fully outstretched in a flexed-foot position. Keep your belly button in, and don't let your lower back arch.

4. Pull your legs back to the starting position. Roll back down one vertebra at a time, switching legs. Repeat 6 times.

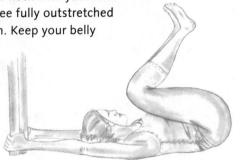

Figure 5.8.
Roll your spine like a baby
having its diaper changed.

ASHLEY'S TIP: To make this more advanced, do it as a straight-leg rollback. Start with your legs straight up in the air at a 90-degree angle and your feet flexed. Stack one foot on top of the other sideways. Inhale, push through your heels, and roll back to pike (baby diaper) position. Exhale, and roll down one vertebra at a time, bringing your legs down as far as you can while still controlling your lower abs. Don't let your lower back arch. Repeat 6 times. This is also a deep hamstring stretch, so don't be alarmed if you feel it in your hamstrings.

Side Planks

1. Lie on your right side with your right elbow directly underneath your right shoulder and your right palm flat on the floor (Figure 5.9). Wrap your left arm around the bottom side of your waist, as if you have a stomachache. Keep your belly in, and fire (contract) your quads. Your feet should be stacked on top of each other, flexed.
2. Exhale, and push your torso away from the ground with your body in a straight line. Bring your torso back down to the starting position. Repeat 5 times on both sides.

ASHLEY'S TIP: To make this more challenging, start in the same position but with your left hand behind your left ear. Push up to the top. Hold. Twist your left elbow down toward your right elbow. Return your elbow back to the starting position. Bring your body down.

Figure 5.9. Keep your body in a straight line for side planks.

Hairwash -

1. Lie down on your back with your hands interlaced behind your head.
2. Bring both shoulder blades off the ground, keeping your eyes on your chest.
3. Pull one knee in toward your belly button with a flexed foot. Extend the other leg out straight. Rotate your elbow to the outside of the opposite knee, and exhale. Hold for 5 seconds.
4. Rotate toward the opposite side, keeping your eyes on your chest and holding your neck still. Allow your hands to move from ear to ear behind your head as you rotate, as if you were washing the back of your hair (Figure 5.10). Repeat 6 times.

Figure 5.10.
Allow your hands
to move behind
your head in
the hairwash.

ASHLEY'S TIP: If you feel this in your lower back or hip flexors, keep your feet lifted higher as you rotate.

Waist Whittler

1. Lie on your back with your arms extended out, elbows slightly bent and palms up.
2. Rest your calves on an exercise ball or bend knees with your legs at a 90-degree angle. Flex your feet with your heels lightly pressing down into the ball (if using). Inhale deeply.
3. Exhale as you drop your knees at a 90-degree angle toward the left side. Aim slightly up toward your armpit as you slowly bring your knees to the side, keeping your abs contracted, shoulders pinned to the floor, and eyes on your chest (Figure 5.11).
4. Return to the starting position. Alternate sides. Repeat 6 times.

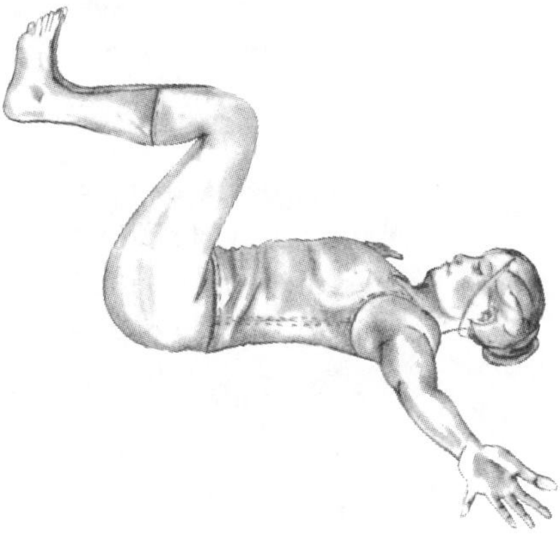

Figure 5.11.
Bring your knees to the side in the waist whittler.

Karate Punch and Twist -

1. Start in athletic stance, and set your spine.
2. Pull your left arm back to a 90-degree angle with your fist facing upward. Simultaneously, cross your right arm across your body with your fist facing downward as if you're doing a karate punch (Figure 5.12). Keep your eyes focused forward. Pause and hold.
3. Alternate sides, punching and then pausing and holding. Exhale with each rotation. Repeat 10 times.

ASHLEY'S TIP: To maximize the burn in your waist, make sure your glutes stay fired and your belly is pulled in.

Figure 5.12.
Release aggression with the karate punch and twist.

ABS-SOLUTELY IMPORTANT TO REMEMBER

No matter how caught up you get in looking good and having six-pack abs, don't forget to focus on your center—your core—and how important it is for everyday movements. Your body is so much more than the sum of its parts. Treat it with respect, and focus on your core for strength, stability, and sexiness.

6

No Butts About It

How to Shape, Tone, and Flatter Your Rear

*T*he booty elicits more negativity than almost any other body part—and we can't even see it without doing contortions in front of the mirror. Luckily, there are so many ways to make your derriere look good that you'll *wish* it were front and center.

BUTT FIRST . . .

When we try on a pair of pants or jeans, the first question that many of us ask is, "Do these make my butt look big?" Pants or jeans certainly don't have to. Like a great bra, great jeans can lift, separate, and hold you in place. All the aesthetics of what we wear on the bottom—the seam work, the pockets, the colors—can make your fanny look fantastic.

Whether you have a flat, wide, narrow, or booty-licious butt, jeans and pants can look amazing on your bottom if you follow some of our fashion and fitness tips to accentuate your body.

If you feel you have a flat butt, *do* wear:

- **Back pockets with a flap:** The best way to enhance a flatter butt is to wear back pockets with flaps. The additional bulk of the flap adds shape to your behind, while the height of the flap draws the eye upward, making your butt appear perkier. The same rule applies for pants, jeans, or skirts.

● **Mermaid skirts with bell- or tulip-shaped bottoms:** When choosing skirts, try to find one that has shape in the back to give you some extra curves.

● **Bustles:** Don't relegate skirt bustles to the late nineteenth century. Bustles add punch to your trunk, especially when you wear long skirts or dresses.

> **PAIGE SAYS:** A bustle is extra padding or framework added to the back of a dress or skirt to create a more rounded or fuller appearance.

● **Belted sweaters:** Long sweaters worn with a belt around the waist pump up the volume on your backside. The cinching in of the belt and the extra thickness of its width create more shape on your back end.

> **PAIGE'S TIP:** Pair a belted sweater with skinny jeans for maximum butt shaping!

● **Peacoats:** Classic wool coats that hit mid-thigh mask a flat butt because of their A-line shape—always a classic winner.

If you feel you have a flat butt, *don't* wear:

● **Pants or skirts without back pockets:** Your backside will look like a flat, blank canvas.

● **Sheath dresses:** These shapeless garments don't add any shape to your rear and are best left alone.

> **PAIGE SAYS:** Sheath dresses are narrow and straight, made popular in the 1950s and 1960s. They may be slightly fitted through the waist.

● **Loose, trouser-style pants:** Pants in thin or wimpy fabrics that fall straight from the waist will hang off your frame and do nothing for you. Look for pants with denser fabrics and more structure to enhance your butt.

● **Small pockets without details or embroidery:** Avoid plain pockets, which add nothing to your trunk.

If you think you have a well-rounded booty, *do* wear:

● **Higher rises:** Pants, jeans, or skirts with higher rises give you ample rear coverage—a must!

● **A-line or bell skirts:** The looser fit of these skirts look great on your bootylicious bottom and can downplay the junk in your trunk if you so choose.

● **Besom or flapped besom pockets:** These slit-shaped pockets look amazing on you because of their high placement and thin construction. Since the pocket is only a slit, it doesn't add any bulk to your backside (Figure 6.1).

Figure 6.1.
Besom pockets are
a good choice.

> **PAIGE SAYS:** ✎ A besom pocket is a flapless pocket that usually graces the front of a men's suit jacket. This pocket is inset and trimmed with a welt that can be anywhere from one-eighth- to one-inch wide.

● **Medium-sized pockets with subtle embroidery:** Look for embroidery in a rounded shape in the same color as your pants to camouflage your bum. Pocket placement here is key. Look for pockets that end where your cheek meets your thigh.

● **Tops that hit the top of your pockets:** Put your best butt forward, and pair it with a top that hits your hip bone or just graces the top of your jeans (Figure 6.2). If you feel you need a little more coverage, then opt for a longer tunic top.

Figure 6.2.
Opt for tops that hit the
top of your pockets.

If you think you have a well-rounded booty, *don't* wear:

- **Large, busy pockets:** You don't want your pockets to have so much action that they attract more attention than a Broadway marquee! Subtle embroidery and minimal decorations are optimal. Likewise, steer clear of large pockets, which accentuate the size of your behind.

- **Tiny pockets:** Itsy-bitsy back pockets leave too much blank space on your backside and can look disproportionate.

PAIGE'S TIP: Back pockets come in all shapes, sizes, and positions, but the most universally flattering placement is when the bottom of the pocket hits where the thigh and the butt cheek meet (Figure 6.3). The pocket shouldn't hit any lower than this or the butt appears droopy.

Figure 6.3.
Tips for perfect
pocket placement.

- **Mermaid-style skirts or skirts with bustles:** The silhouettes of these skirts only amplify your derriere.

- **Wide-wale corduroys:** These and other heavy fabrics pad your tush with more thickness, adding bulk to your booty. Stick to thinner, less bulky fabrics, and thin-wale corduroys.

If you think you have a wide butt, *do* wear:

- **Wide-leg or boot-cut pants or jeans:** The wider bottoms help even out your middle and bottom proportions.

- **Rounded, flapless back pockets:** These give your rear a nice cherry or apple shape.

Figure 6.4.
Look for back-pocket detail
that is high and not too wide.

- **Back pockets with embroidery or details:** Look for embroidery that is high and not too wide (Figure 6.4). You want the eye to look vertically up and down, not across horizontally. The shape of the embroidery can focus the eye inward.

- **Skirts with ruching or seams:** Ruching in the middle of the butt or skirts with center back seams narrow your backside.

- **Vertical stripes:** Pinstripes or other vertical patterns on skirts, pants, or longer tunic tops help elongate the look of the butt.

- **High-rise pants and jeans:** The higher rise emphasizes the waist, not just the booty, and elongates that area instead of widening it.

- **Long, narrow skirts and dresses:** These longer bottoms help lengthen the body and detract the focus from your backside (Figure 6.5).

- **Bermuda and capri shorts:** Longer shorts help lengthen your look, bringing less attention to the bum area.

If you think you have a wide butt, *don't* wear:

- **Short, wide back pockets:** These only make your butt look wider, instead of narrowing it. Wide backside + wide pockets = fashion don't.

- **Wide back-pocket embroidery:** The horizontal designs accentuate the width of your derriere. Look for narrower, vertical embroidery instead.

- **Low rises:** Pants or skirts with lower rises can make you look compact and wide since there's no focus on your smaller waist. Remember to accentuate your best assets.

- **Miniskirts and short shorts:** Short skirts, especially minis, and very short shorts can make you look boxy from the back.

- **Horizontal stripes:** Wearing these only emphasizes your width.

Figure 6.5.
Do wear long, narrow dresses and skirts to lengthen the body.

If you feel you have a narrow butt, *do* wear:

- **Lower-rise jeans, pants, and skirts:** The lower rise gives the illusion of a wider derriere.

- **Belted jackets or blouses:** Longer jackets and blouses that hit below the butt cheeks can add more width and shape to your lower half.

  PAIGE'S TIP: These look particularly good when belted, giving you an A-line shape on the bottom.

- **Back pockets with horizontal detailing:** Look for embroidery or insignias that are more horizontal in design to broaden your booty.

- **Miniskirts and short shorts:** The shorter, boxier lines help broaden the backside (Figure 6.6).

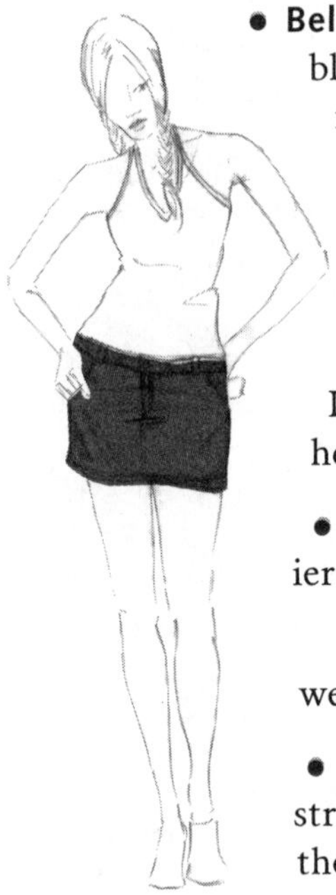

If you feel you have a narrow butt, *don't* wear:

- **Vertical stripes:** Try to stay away from vertical stripes, like pinstripes, across your booty, because the verticality makes you look narrower.

- **Long pockets:** Pockets that are too long and skinny on your backside just lend a narrower, not fuller, look in general.

Figure 6.6.
Do wear miniskirts.

BUTT WHAT ABOUT ME?

There's more to the bum than shape alone. Other pesky conditions, such as sagging and cellulite, can rear their ugly heads. We've got fashion solutions for those too, but look ahead to "The Moves" section for fitness tips on how to correct, and not just mask, them. If we don't work out our butt muscles (our glutes), our butts *will* sag over time. Gravity is a powerful force. When your butt starts to sag, follow these easy fixes for an instant butt-lift.

If you have a sagging butt, *do* wear:

- **Jeans with color highlights on top:** Wearing lighter shades close to your waistband *above* your pocket draws the eye up so your butt actually looks higher.

> **PAIGE'S TIP:** ✏ Watch out for highlights that are too extreme—they'll make you look like you sat on some white paint!

- **Jeans that are 2 percent Lycra and 98 percent cotton:** This mixture of cotton and Lycra, especially in a nice tight-weave fabric that's more fitted through the hip and thigh area, helps lift and separate your bum as if it were a butt bra.

> **PAIGE'S TIP:** ✏ Be careful that there isn't *too* much Lycra (more than 2 percent) or the texture can be too spongy and won't hold you up at all. The fabric may start to ripple like a pair of leggings. Also, if there isn't ample cotton (at least 98 percent), then there won't be enough structure to hold you up.

- **Trousers with flap pockets:** Look for trousers in nice woven fabrics that have back-flap pockets. The pockets draw the eye up, giving you more bulk where you need it, while the characteristics of the fabric help boost your booty.

If you have a sagging butt, *don't* wear:

- **Low pockets:** Make sure the bottoms of the back pockets don't extend lower than your butt cheeks. The lower pockets only make your butt look saggier.

THE C WORD

Chances are, you have butt dimples. Most of us have them. Even supermodels have cellulite—they just have a team of fabulous photographers who airbrush every photo. Wouldn't that be nice! But magically erasing our flaws isn't realistic. Even if you feel like you have more cottage cheese than a grocery store, try to remember that the way you store fat is genetic. Women tend to store fat in their butt and thighs, resulting in larger fat cells in those areas, which push up against the connective tissue and cause dimpling. Here are some tips that give the illusion of instant airbrushing.

If you have a dimply butt, *do* wear:

IN YOUR JEANS

*J*eans can be so flattering if you find the right pair for your body type. If you're generally body-conscious and don't want to wear anything tight or figure-enhancing, look for boyfriend-style, looser-fitting jeans that sit low on your hips. They should drape, not cling to you, and look like they're a size larger than you need—then you definitely won't draw attention to your booty. They can be straight-leg or even skinny jeans, but try to wear an empire-waist babydoll top or a blazer over a button-down that hits where your cheek and butt meet. You get a great, long, leggy look with no attention to your bum.

• **Jeans that are 2 percent Lycra and 98 percent cotton or jeans with polyester blends:** The composition of the fabric is a plus for you and holds your butt in.

> **PAIGE'S TIP:** Look for heavier denim. The thicker, tighter weave sucks and holds you in, masking any ripples. Don't be fooled by magic fixes such as "anticellulite jeans" that claim to reduce cellulite the longer you wear them. If that were true, we'd eat, sleep, and shower in them.

• **Undies with Lycra or spandex:** These undergarments hold in your rear much more effectively than a G-string or thong.

If you have a dimply butt, *don't* wear:

• **Sheer fabrics:** Avoid these at all costs, unless you want every bump, dot, and dimple on display. Nude, beige, or white sheer fabrics are particularly revealing. You might feel overexposed!

WORKING THE BACKSIDE

Most of us don't have jobs climbing mountains. In fact, we're more likely to be sitting at our desks all day long. When we don't actively train our glutes, our muscles atrophy and we end up with wide, flat butts—and we wonder why our backsides look like deflated balloons!

One reason many of us don't work out our glutes is simply fear. We're afraid that working them out in the wrong way may accidentally make them—or us—look bigger. Yes, sometimes when we start weight training, our jeans start to fit differently and can pull across the tops of our thighs. But don't let that discourage you. If you're working your glutes and developing toned half-moon-shaped cheeks, your muscles may temporarily swell for the first couple of days because of a buildup of lactic acid. Keep working out! The swelling will go down, and you'll look and feel fabulous.

Also, there's *risk* in not working out your glutes. When you don't have a strong bottom half, your core has to go into overdrive to compensate for it. Aesthetically, you'll start to look more quad-dominant with more muscles in the front of your legs and flatter glutes and hamstrings. The glutes can atrophy and collect more cellulite, becoming mushy and spreading out wider.

You don't have to spot-train your glutes to get benefits. The glutes are affected by your quads, hamstrings, and calves, so working the glutes involves working other areas too. Try to think about your legs as one powerful engine, and do biomechanically correct moves (like those that follow) that will help your body the most. Here are a few FAQs to put you on the right track.

• **Will doing the StairMaster every day bulk up my butt?** Any repetitive motion builds up certain muscles because you're hitting the same muscle group over and over again. Always rotate your cardio machines. Try doing an hour of cardio: twenty minutes each on three different machines. Using multiple machines works your legs and glutes at different angles, targeting various muscle groups.

• **Can I reverse gravity, or am I doomed to have a sagging butt?** You can aid in reversing the gravitational pull. Weight training thwarts gravity's game plan by preventing the loss of muscle mass. The more aware you are of your body in day-to-day life and as you train, the quicker it will respond.

• **Do certain exercises reduce cellulite?** Cellulite usually occurs when there's excess body fat, which can be reduced by the right combination of food, water, cardio, and weight training. Cardio helps by burning the fat off, while weight training builds the underlying muscle groups, increasing your metabolism. The most effective exercises are compound movements, which involve using two or more muscle groups in one exercise. To have a lean body, be conscious of what food you're eating (see Chapter 10) and drink a minimum of 64 ounces of water a day.

You'll need:

- A yoga or gym mat
- A softball or squash ball

Training Guidelines

1. Do all of the following eight moves in the order provided:
   - Cowboy rolls
   - Split squats
   - Single-leg heel press
   - Static side lunge
   - Active pigeon stretch
   - Speed skater jumps
   - Step-ups
   - Sumo squats
2. Repeat the sequence two to three times, back-to-back.
3. Do this workout two to three times a week.

ASHLEY'S TIP: Do the hips series first to warm up the area. (See Chapter 7.)

The Moves

These biomechanically correct moves will tone your tush in no time.

Cowboy Rolls

1. Lie down on your back, and bend both knees with your feet flat on the floor. Keep your elbows by your sides, hands resting lightly on your stomach. Cross your right ankle over your left knee like a cowboy, and put a softball or squash ball under your right glute.

Figure 6.7.
Rock back and forth
sitting like a cowboy.

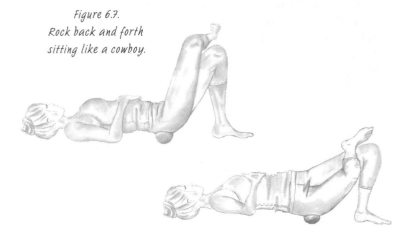

2. Bring your left knee toward the ground, and slowly roll back and forth for 2 minutes (Figure 6.7). Switch legs and repeat.

Split Squats

1. Start in athletic stance, and set your spine. Take a giant step back with your right foot (Figure 6.8). Keep your weight evenly distributed between both feet. Squeeze the glute of your back leg, and contract your pelvic muscles.

2. Slowly bend both knees down to a 90-degree angle in a lunge position. Your back knee should not touch the ground.

   ASHLEY'S TIP: Your feet should *not* be directly in front of each other as if you were balanced on a tightrope. Instead, your legs should be hip-width apart, and you should not be able to see your heels in the mirror.

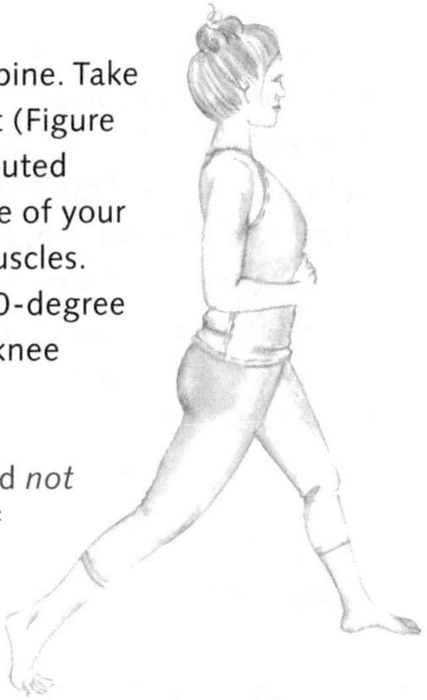

3. Hold and squeeze your back glute. You should feel a huge stretch in

Figure 6.8.
Keep your legs hip-width
apart for split squats.

your right leg. Push up to the
top of the split squat. Repeat
10 times with each leg.

ASHLEY'S TIP:  To make
this more challenging, do a
step-back split squat. Start
in athletic stance. Step back
directly into lunge position.
Drop down, come up, and step
forward. Return to the starting
position. Repeat.

Single-Leg Heel Press --

1. Lie on your back with your elbows at a 90-degree angle. Your triceps should be pressed into the floor with your fingertips reaching to the ceiling.
2. Put the arches of both feet on the edge of a stable surface, hip-
   width apart, with your knees bent. Press through your feet.
   Squeeze your glutes.
3. Raise your hips off the ground
   to the top of a bridge position (Figure 6.9). Your body
   should form a straight line
   from your knees to your
   shoulders.

Figure 6.9.
Keep your hips raised in
a bridge position for the
single-leg heel press.

4. Extend your left leg straight out with your foot flexed, keeping your knees in line with each other. Bring your leg back down to the bridge position. Never let your back sag. Return to the starting position. Alternating legs, repeat 10 times.

Static Side Lunge

1. Stand with your feet a foot (12 inches) wider than athletic stance, and set your spine. Interlace your hands below your rib cage.
2. Slowly bending your right knee, sit back with your right glute as if you were going to sit in a chair (Figure 6.10). As you sit back, keep your left leg straight and fire the quad. Make sure your feet face forward.

Figure 6.10.
You shouldn't see your heels
when doing static side lunges.

ASHLEY'S TIP: The weight of both feet should be placed between your first and second toes and the outside edge of your heels. You should not be able to see your heels in the mirror.

3. Hold for two counts. Return to the starting position. Repeat 10 times with each leg.

Active Pigeon Stretch

1. Start at the top of a push-up position with your feet hip-width apart, your elbows on the ground.

2. Bend your right knee, and bring it forward on the ground under the outer edge of your right armpit (Figure 6.11). Try to aim your right toe at a 90-degree angle under your left armpit.

3. Bring your left knee down to the ground and really tuck your toes under, pushing down to the ground. Pull your belly button in.

4. Push back through your left heel, raising your knee off the ground. Squeeze your left glute. Hold for 10 seconds. Bring the knee back down. Repeat 5 times with each leg.

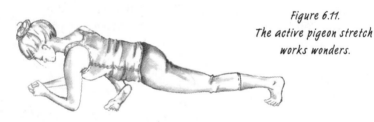

Figure 6.11.
The active pigeon stretch
works wonders.

Speed Skater Jumps

1. Start in athletic stance. Keep your elbows at your sides with your hands slightly in front of your body, like a wrestler. Focus on a nonmoving object directly in front of you.

2. Cross your right foot behind your left leg with both knees slightly bent, keeping your belly button in.

Figure 6.12.
Act like an Olympian
doing speed
skater jumps.

3. Pressing off from the big toe and outside heel of your left foot, jump out to the right side just farther than athletic-stance width (Figure 6.12). Land toe-ball-heel on your right foot, bending your knees slightly and keeping the weight in your back heel. Cross your left foot slightly behind your right leg.
4. Jump to the other side. Use your back foot to push off and jump to the other side. Repeat 10 times.

Step-Ups

1. Start in athletic stance. Face a stable platform surface at the height of a fitness bench. Place your left foot on top of the bench. Keep your feet separated at the same width as you raise your foot.
2. As you step up, pull your belly button in and fire your left glute (Figure 6.13). Bring your right hand up, keeping your elbow by your side.
3. While you're pushing through the heel of your left leg, bring the right foot up. At the top of the move, your eyes should be on the horizon, your left hand up with the elbow at your side, and your right hand down by your legs.

ASHLEY'S TIP: Touch only the ball of your right foot on the step (a "pageant foot," as if you were in a beauty pageant). Keep all the weight on your left foot. Your spine should stay straight as if a broom is running vertically along your spine.

4. Step back with the ball of your right foot, bringing your eyes down to the floor in front of you. Plant your heel on the ground, and fire your glute. Bring the left leg back to the starting position. Repeat 10 times with each leg.

ASHLEY'S TIP: To make this move more challenging for your glutes, keep your hands interlaced against your tummy throughout the exercise.

Figure 6.13.
Step up carefully on the
ball of your foot with
weight on your left foot.

Sumo Squats ---

1. Start with your legs 4 inches wider apart than in athletic stance. Set your spine, contract your glutes, and pull your belly in.
2. Slowly descend at medium pace to a deep squat, as if you're sitting in a low chair. Keep your weight evenly distributed on both feet. Your ears, hips, and spine should be perpendicular to the floor. Don't let your knees collapse inward when you descend into the squat.
3. Return to the starting position at the same medium pace. Repeat 10 times.

ASHLEY'S TIP: To make this more challenging, interlace your hands behind your head and slightly push your head back into your palms (Figure 6.14). Keep your elbows reaching out to opposite sides of the room. Don't push your neck forward.

Figure 6.14.
Keep your hands
interlaced to make this
move more challenging.

MAKING THE BOOTY AN ASS-ET

Now that you're in touch with the power and beauty of the booty, the key to success is consistency and lack of fear. Try all of our different fashion and fitness tips, and have fun. Remember, we are all works-in-progress. Plant an "under construction" sign across your tush, and get moving. We all can strengthen and shape our bums, so get out there and kick some ass.

7

Your Hips Don't Lie

Slimming Tips for Hips

*W*hen we hear women frantically wail, "Help, I have huge hips!" we know it's the result of several possible factors:

- Excess body fat can make your hips, and everything else, appear larger.
- When your glutes start to spread from lack of use (see Chapter 6), your hips start to look wider.
- The size of your hips is based on the positioning of your hip bones. If you have widely spaced hip bones, then you'll always have wider hips, no matter how in shape you are. However, having narrow hip bones doesn't mean you're a toned goddess. Narrow hips can still be covered in a layer of fat and need proper exercise.
- Simply put, we're women. We carry more body fat around our hips than in most other areas, thanks to our evolutionary function as child bearers. (Don't hate men for having narrow hips—that's the way they are built.) We are meant to have curves because we're meant to be givers of life—it's really a blessing! As women we should embrace the beautiful curves and silhouette of our bodies.

HIPSTER TIPS

That *doesn't* mean we're stuck with the hips we have. Our fashion and fitness tips for wide and narrow hips help strengthen and shape your hips while accentuating your natural, womanly contours.

If you think your hips are too wide, *do* wear:

● **L-shaped front pockets:** These more angular pockets draw the eye inward and away from the hips. This type of opening gives a trouser feel without having pockets that sit too far out on the hips.

> **PAIGE SAYS:** ⯈ L-shaped pockets sit under the waistband of a skirt or pant. When viewed from the side, the pocket forms the letter *L*.

> **PAIGE'S TIP:** ⯈ If your pants have side pockets that gape open, take them to a tailor or dry cleaner and have them sewn shut. They sit more smoothly on your hips, and who uses those pockets anyway?

● **Classic-rise pants with a wider waistband:** The wide dimension on the top of the pants masks the extra width around your hips. This waistband style also helps smooth out the area between the waist and hips, giving you a curvy, sexy shape.

> **PAIGE SAYS:** ⯈ The rise is the distance between the crotch and the waist of a garment. A classic rise is timeless. Most classic rises fall about one inch below the belly button.

● **Boot-cut five-pocket jeans:** The ever-so-slight flare at the bottom of these classic-rise jeans balances out your hips (Figure 7.1). The front pocket placement and shape hits you in just the right places.

● **Wide belt loops:** Jeans with wide belt loops (the first loop starting away from the center) or with design details close to the front zipper draw more attention to your middle instead of to your hips.

● **A-line or tulip-shaped skirts:** The fuller opening at the bottom of these skirts balances out your hips and thighs (Figure 7.2).

- **Skirts that fall at or below the knee:** Skirts at this length elongate the body and take the spotlight off your hips. These are particularly sexy on fuller hips, but beware of bias-cut fabric. Go for a densely woven fabric in a straight cut.

- **Raglan-sleeve tops:** Any top that helps broaden your shoulders is a wise choice. The more width there is to your shoulders, the more balanced and in proportion your hips appear.

- **Tunics:** The soft, draped coverage of tunic-style blouses, knits, and sweaters helps hide any unwanted inches around the hip area.

- **A-line jackets and coats:** Go for outerwear such as a belted peacoat. The most flattering length hits at your calf or below your knee because this elongates and creates balance in your body.

Figure 7.1.
Five-pocket jeans
balance out your hips.

- **Shoulder details:** Shoulder pads, slightly puffed sleeves, and epaulets on jackets help distract attention from your hips by highlighting your shoulders instead.

If you think your hips are too wide, *don't* wear:

- **Traditional front trouser pockets (horizontal slot pockets):** These rounded shapes tend to gape open and make you look wider than you are.

- **Pockets with flaps:** At all costs, avoid wearing pants pockets with flaps on the front, back, or sides. The added fabric from the flaps only adds bulk to your frame.

Figure 7.2.
This fun, flirty tulip-shaped
skirt will flare just right.

• **Tapered jeans:** Jeans that are too tapered at the bottom can emphasize the width of your hip area.

> **PAIGE'S TIP:** ⤳ Try tucking skinny jeans into boots and pairing them with a long tunic or blazer to balance out your proportions.

• **High-waisted jeans:** High-waisted jeans can be your worst enemy, especially if you have a small waist. The higher rise only accentuates, rather than hides, curves.

• **Pencil skirts:** These slim skirts in form-fitting fabrics cling to your body all the way down. The tighter and thinner the fabric, the more the skirt reveals your hips. And if it's cut on the bias, it'll cling to you as if there's no tomorrow.

• **Fan pleating:** Skirts with pleats all the way around have so much extra fabric it'll look like there's another you! Puffy and pouf skirts also have the tendency to add more to you than necessary.

• **Narrow tops:** Any top that is too narrow through the shoulders inadvertently draws attention to your hips. Instead of spaghetti straps, wear wider straps to even out your proportions.

• **Short tops:** The best length for you is at or below the hip bone. If the top is too short, your hips will be front and center.

• **Horizontal lines:** Lines that run across the body only make you look wider.

• **Cropped or bolero-style jackets:** These sit above the waistline and cut your torso in the wrong place instead of elongating your body.

If you think your hips are too narrow, *do* wear:

• **Front slant pockets:** Pants or trousers with front slant pockets work great on you because the angular placement of the pockets makes your hips look wider.

> **PAIGE'S TIP:** ⤳ Those of you with narrow hips are lucky because you can wear any style of pants or skirts with side zippers.

• **Front pleats:** Pants with front pleats amplify your hip area. The fuller the fabric, the fuller you'll look.

- **Skinny peg-legged jeans:** These carrot-shaped jeans, which taper tightly at the ankle, look great on you (Figure 7.3). No need to stuff them into boots. Go for a pair of ballet flats or sexy heels to show off the taper.

- **High-waisted jeans:** Your hips look more voluptuous if you accentuate your smaller waist.

- **Pleated skirts:** Have fun with pleats, pleats, and more pleats! These folds, in any shape and style, help add dimension to your middle. Bubble and pouf skirts also look great on you.

- **Layers:** Tank tops, tunics, and turtlenecks that hit at or below your waist look amazing under vests that hit just above your hip bones. This look creates volume and shape at the same time.

- **Low-slung belts:** Low-slung belts on your hips over tunics, blouses, or sweaters are a win-win. The loose-fitting top paired with the bulkier belt adds dimension in just the right spot.

- **Jackets and blazers with peplums:** These are a nice choice for you, especially if you're into 1940s glamour. The small waistline paired with the fullness across your hips makes your body look bodacious (Figure 7.4).

- **Double-breasted trench coats:** Trench coats that hit above the knee can be fun and sleek at the same time. Tighten the belt as much as you want to cinch in your waist without worrying about your hips; the extra volume of the coat gives the illusion of curvier hips.

Figure 7.3.
Skinny peg-legged jeans are perfect for narrow hips.

Figure 7.4.
Peplum on blazers looks amazing!

PAIGE'S TIP: If you want to accentuate your hips (and don't mind breaking a fingernail or two), go for button-fly closures. If you prefer not to have any extra bulk in your middle, opt for a zip fly, which gives you a flatter front. If you have narrower hips, you can get away with side and back zippers, but make sure you still maintain your curves.

If you think your hips are too narrow, *don't* wear:

- **Pants without detailing:** If your pants have no detailing across the front (no pockets, zippers, or designs), your hips look even narrower. Avoid center back zippers and pants without front pockets.

- **Straight pants:** Pants that fall down from your hips with no shape at all make you look even straighter. To add curves, look for more shapely structured trousers.

- **Bell-shaped or flared jeans:** Your hips go bye-bye in these jeans, which bring the emphasis down the leg.

- **Front patch pockets:** Jeans with front patch pockets that sit too close to the zipper only draw the eye inward and give the illusion of narrower hips.

- **Straight skirts:** Skirts where the lines of the garment fall straight down from your hips give you an ultra-aligned shape that only makes your body look straighter.

- **Vertical lines:** Prints or fabrics with vertical lines, such as pinstripe patterns or corduroys, only elongate your frame by bringing the eye from head to toe in one direction.

- **Loose tops:** Loose-fitting tops that skim the body can engulf your frame and further hide your hips.

- **Busy tops:** Tops with too much action across the shoulders bring the focus up. Anything that makes your shoulders look puffier or broader makes your hips look slimmer.

- **Shapeless jackets and coats:** Coats that fall straight down without adding shape only draw out your figure. You'll look long and lean, but you won't have any curves.

- **Large lapels:** Jackets and blazers with really large lapels add too much breadth across the shoulders and chest area, making your hips look smaller.

TRYING TO BE TOO HIP

Despite the saying, many of us do judge a book by its cover. What we wear is one of the first things people notice about us. With all that pressure, it can be tempting to rely heavily on the latest trends as a quick and safe fix. That strategy can backfire when you find yourself wearing outfits that are "in" but don't flatter your figure or express who you are. For example, tweens can pull off wearing hip-huggers (i.e., pants, skirts, or jeans where the waistline wraps around the hipbone) thanks to their youthful physiques and narrow hips, but the rest of us are better off with higher-rise pants.

Remember, you can be fashionable without being a fashionista. Dress for *your* body and *your* age. Even if you're forty and fabulous, stick to age-appropriate attire to look your best. Be proud of your age, and age gracefully—don't fight it. If you're young, don't dress matronly just to be taken seriously, and if you're in your sixties, don't dress as if you're still in your twenties.

Also, always consider what you're doing to your body and how reversible it is. You can remove a belly button ring, but a tattoo is a little tougher. When making decisions, remember that beauty is timeless, ageless, and classic, and dressing to reflect who you are beats any current fad.

HIP TO BE SQUARE

Our hips sure take a beating. We sit for hours on end with our legs crossed at our desks, in our cars, and while traveling. We run around town in heels, pounding on the pavement, or wear shoes such as flip-flops and flats that have no support at all. Of course we're bound to feel a little hip pain!

But the discomfort doesn't necessarily stop with our hips. Our lower body functions like a machine. Not taking care of one part throws a wrench in the system and eventually leads to a body breakdown. Lower-back and shoulder pain rear their ugly heads. Here are a few common culprits and what you can do about them.

• **Sitting with crossed legs:** When we sit like this for long periods of time, our ligaments start to overstretch and lose their alignment. It's like sitting with a band across our laps and a heavy weight pulling down one side of it. Over time, the band stretches out. When this happens to our hips, our bodies try to correct the damage by overexerting other areas (e.g., the lower back and shoulders), which begin to hurt from all the extra work. Also, the underused muscles, such as the quads, start to get really tight. Sitting in an ergonomically correct position can help.

• **Traveling:** Sitting in a cramped, compromised position doesn't help our muscles or circulation. When flying, don't be afraid to use your carry-on bag as a footstool so your hips can stay aligned. Try to get up and walk around as much as possible. Fold a blanket or use a pillow to support your lower back.

• **Shoes:** Wearing four-inch heels is a recipe for disaster. The concrete street pavement and hard floors of your office are so unforgiving. Your body has to work extra hard to maintain balance and alignment. Don't be surprised if you get shin splints and hip or lower-back pain. Flats with no arch support, such as flip-flops, can be equally detrimental since they provide no protection. Look for a pair of comfortable walking or running shoes instead. (Those ladies who wear their sneaks to work and change in the lobby are the smart ones.) If you just can't bear to walk around in running shoes, opt for wedges, shoes with cork or rubber soles, sandals with two straps on top, or flats that have built-in arch support, instead of torturing yourself in high heels.

Most of all, listen to your body. If you start feeling pain, your body is trying to tell you something. By following these exercises, you'll not only strengthen your hips, but you'll also prevent pain—and look better too!

ROLL WITH IT

One of the most effective ways to improve the appearance of your hips is by rolling out (see the following first two moves). Think of your legs as a piece of uncooked brisket. Before you put the meat in the oven, it's a hunk of solid muscle. Once it cooks, it becomes stringy in texture. Rolling out your legs does the same thing. The muscles warm up and the ligaments separate, allowing more blood to pump through your body, thereby increasing your metabolic rate. It's a deeper move than just stretching, because it kicks your whole body into gear.

You'll need:

- A yoga or gym mat
- A foam roller or PVC pipe from your local home-improvement store (approximately 3 feet by 4 inches, available at relaxtheback.com)
- A small, weighted ball (1,000 grams/2.2 pounds, 5-inch diameter, such as Fitball's Heavymed ball, available at performbetter.com or power-systems.com)

SPINNING YOUR WHEELS

Spinning (i.e., exercising in a group on stationary bikes) is an extremely popular form of cardio. Spinning addicts love how much the classes make them sweat and how many calories they burn. But spinning may not be your best bet, especially if you already spend most of your time sitting at a desk.

Sitting on a spinning bike is almost identical to sitting in a chair, only you're tilted forward. The dreaded "computer body syndrome" will persist and get more aggravated. Yes, you'll build up your quads, but you can also come down with "deflated spinning butt" since you won't be working your glutes or stretching your hips.

If you adore spinning, have your instructor check that you're using proper form, and be sure to supplement your routine with hip and glute stretching and strengthening moves.

Training Guidelines

1. Do all of the following six moves in the order provided:
   - Military crawl
   - Cleopatra roll
   - Psoas release
   - Softball pose
   - Active lying-down hip stretch
   - Lying-down hip series
2. Repeat all the moves consecutively (this is the hips series) two to three times, back-to-back.
3. Do this workout two to three times a week.

The Moves

Your hips won't lie when you're working them out with these killer exercises.

Military Crawl --

1. Lie facedown on a mat. Prop yourself up on your forearms, and extend your legs directly behind you in a straight line. Relax your feet.
2. Place a foam roller underneath your legs across the center of your thighs. Keep your head in line with your spine, your eyes facing downward. Pull in your belly.
3. Slowly crawl forward on your forearms (like a soldier in boot camp) up to the top of your thighs (Figure 7.5). Then crawl backward to just above your kneecaps so your toes barely touch the floor. Repeat 5 times.

Figure 7.5.
Slowly crawl forward as
if you're in the military.

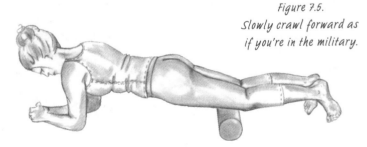

119

4. Turn your feet out so your heels are together and your toes are apart. Repeat the crawl 5 times.
5. Turn your feet in so your toes are together and your heels are apart (i.e., pigeon-toed). Repeat the crawl 5 times.

ASHLEY'S TIP: If you feel any pain or knotting in your leg as you crawl, pull your belly button in, place the opposite (not-hurting) foot on the floor, and then bend and extend the leg 2 to 3 times to loosen it.

Cleopatra Roll

1. Lie down on your side with your hips stacked on top of each other. Prop yourself up on your bottom forearm, extending your legs back in a straight line.
2. Keep your head in line with your spine, eyes facing downward, belly button pulled in, feet straight and relaxed.
3. Place the roller under the middle of your bottom thigh. Your top leg is bent with your foot on the ground slightly in front of you. Your bottom leg is fully extended underneath you.
4. While pushing away from the floor with your top foot, slowly roll up toward the top of your hip (Figure 7.6). Then roll back down to just above your kneecap. Repeat 5 times slowly. Bend and extend the top leg 5 times.

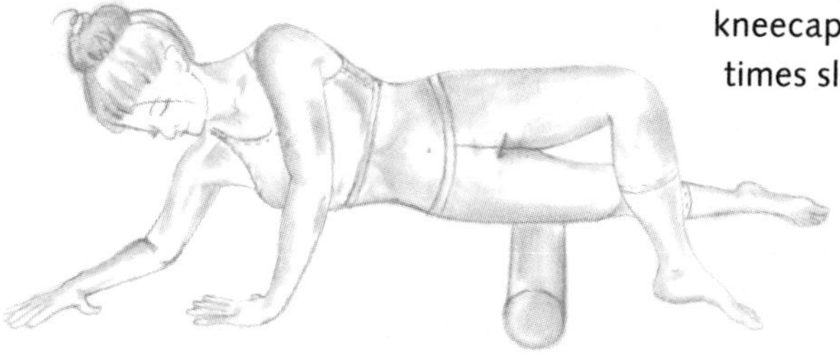

Figure 7.6. Roll up and back for the Cleopatra roll.

ASHLEY'S TIP: Don't end up in a shrimp position. If you look at your legs throughout the crawl, your spine will curve. Keep your eyes forward and in line with your spine.

Psoas Release

1. Put your right thumb on your belly button. Extend your right pinky out to your hip bone. Mark the middle of that line with your finger.
2. Lie facedown on a mat with a slightly weighted ball underneath you on that spot (Figure 7.7). Keep your arms at your sides, palms facing up, with your head turned to one side.
3. Hold for 2 minutes, breathing easily. Repeat with the ball on your left side, and hold for 2 minutes.

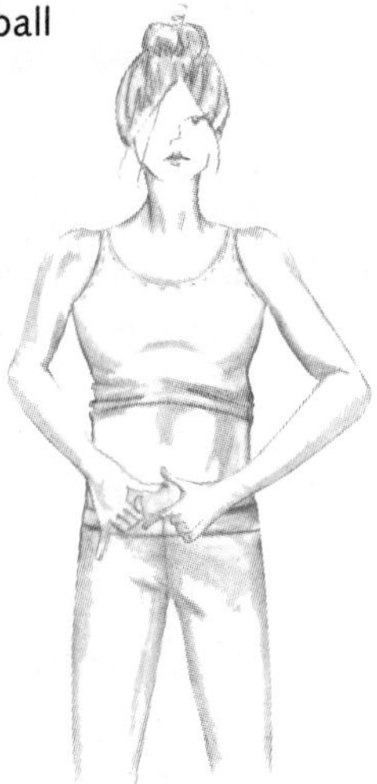

Figure 7.7.
Place a weighted ball
right under this area.

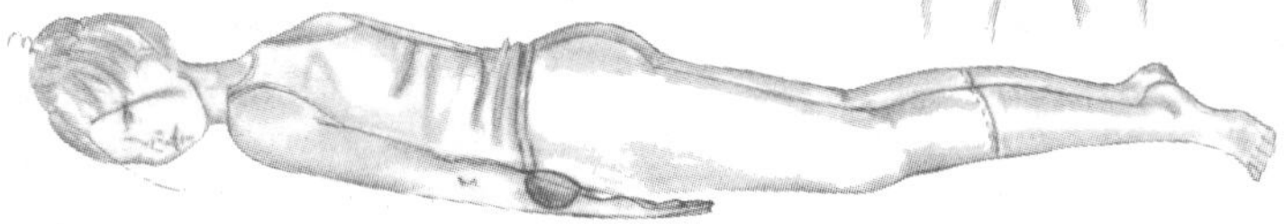

ASHLEY'S TIP: *Don't* do this move during your period or if you're pregnant or might be pregnant.

Softball Pose

1. Kneel on one knee with your front foot flat on the floor at a 90-degree angle (Figure 7.8). Curl the toes of your back foot under, and push down between your first and second toes.

2. Place both hands on your front knee, pull your belly button in, and squeeze the glute of your back leg.
3. Hold for 10 seconds. Switch legs and repeat.

ASHLEY'S TIP: Make sure your knees aren't too close together. When you look in the mirror, your knees should be about hip-width apart—you shouldn't be able to see your back foot. To make this move more advanced, if your right knee is on the ground, extend your right arm straight up to the ceiling with your thumb rotated back, pushing toward the wall behind you. Your left hand should be reaching down and back. Keep your elbows slightly bent and your belly button in. Hold for 10 seconds. Switch legs and arms and repeat.

Figure 7.8. You'll look like you're posing for a team photo with the softball pose.

Active Lying-Down Hip Stretch

1. Lie down on your back with your legs extended out in front of you. Place a small folded-up towel underneath the small protruding bone on the lower half of your skull, your occipital bone.
2. Grab your left knee with your left hand below the kneecap, and pull it toward your left armpit (Figure 7.9). With your right hand, grab your ankle. Pull your ankle toward your right armpit. Block your shoulders down with your elbows pushing out to opposite walls.

Figure 7.9. This deep stretch helps your whole hip area.

3. Flex your right foot and push through
   the right heel, squeezing your glute.
   Hold   for   10 seconds. Switch
   legs and
   repeat.

Lying-Down Hip Series ---------------------------------

Do both parts consecutively while lying on one side. Then switch
sides, and repeat the series.

Part 1

1. Start on your side with your hips stacked on top of each other.
   Your bottom arm is extended out underneath your ear, your belly
   button is pulled in, and your glutes are tight.
2. Place your top arm in front of your chest to stabilize you. Look
   toward your feet. Move your feet behind you a few inches, keeping them in a straight line.
3. Lift your top leg slightly, and flex both feet (Figure 7.10). Slowly
   bring the toes of your top foot down toward the instep of the
   bottom foot in a pigeon-toed position. Tuck in your glutes.

Figure 7.10.
Part 1 of the hips series
involves a kicking motion.

4. Push through your top heel, and raise the top leg up toward the ceiling as high as you can before your back starts to arch, keeping your waist lifted up. Repeat 15 times, slowly.

> **ASHLEY'S TIP:** Don't let the bottom part of your waist fall. Keep it lifted as you bring your leg up. It's a small movement, but you should feel a lot of burn on the outside bottom of your glutes.

Part 2

1. Stay on your side with your hips stacked on top of each other. Bend your bottom knee and bring it slightly forward, belly button in. Flex the foot of your top leg and bend the knee.
2. Bring the top knee in toward your belly button (Figure 7.11). Then push it back out with the top foot flexed, bringing your top leg slightly behind the bottom leg.
3. Squeeze the glute of the top leg, tucking your tush under. Repeat 15 times, slowly.

Figure 7.11.
In part 2, bring your top
knee into your chest.

WORSH-HIP YOUR BODY

We get only one body to live in. Falling victim to some basics of everyday life can be much more detrimental than you might think. Try to maximize the benefits to your body even in something as simple as choosing which shoes to wear.

Thigh High

Sculpting Your Upper Legs to Look Divine

*O*ur thighs are one of the softest, sexiest, shapeliest areas of our bodies. Yet these curvy symbols of femininity can cause such angst. For many, the thigh area conjures up visions of cellulite and stretch marks, not smooth skin or inner power.

It's true that when we gain weight, our thighs tend to take some of the heat. Who hasn't had their thighs rub together when walking or running and felt totally uncomfortable and self-conscious? But wearing the right types of clothes for your thighs can emphasize all that there is to love about them, especially their strength and sensuality. Dressing for your body's proportions is also helpful when showing off your thighs, so keep in mind the length of your legs and torso.

Toning your inner and outer thighs can work wonders for your physique and change or improve your already fit lower body. Now get ready to say good-bye to those old lies about your thighs.

THIGH SUPPLIES

If you feel your thighs are too full or narrow for your physique, follow these tips to dress your best.

If you feel that your thighs are fuller than average, *do* wear:

- **Straight or slightly A-line skirts:** Skirts in darker shades that hit two to three inches above the knee are your best option. Pairing the skirt with heels makes your legs look longer and your thighs look leaner.

- **Mid-thigh shorts:** Shorts that end mid-thigh or lower work great for fuller thighs. The extra fabric exposes less leg, lengthening the thigh-to-knee area. If you opt for the longer shorts, make sure to avoid anything that tapers too much. Straight is great for fuller thighs!

> **PAIGE'S TIP:** If you're trying to hide stretch marks or cellulite around your thighs, wear a cute pair of hose or leggings underneath your shorts.

- **Pants or jeans with a slight flare or boot cut:** The wider bottom of the pant helps create balance with your thighs (Figure 8.1). The pants shouldn't be too tight at the knee.

- **Darker colors on your bottom half and brighter colors around your face:** This color combination accentuates your upper-body assets and takes away any unwanted attention from your thighs.

- **Skirts that are long and flowing:** Anything that doesn't cling to your body is great for covering up your thighs if that's your goal.

- **Tunic-length babydoll shirts and dresses:** The long A-line style of these tops just covers your thighs, making your legs look a mile long.

> **PAIGE'S TIP:** Pair babydoll shirts and dresses with skinny dark jeans and platform shoes for a fantastic slimming look.

Figure 8.1.
Jeans with flare and babydoll tops balance out fuller thighs.

- **Wide-leg or tubular-shaped pants:** The larger measurement of the knee opening balances out the thigh and leg shape, making your legs look longer (Figure 8.2).

PAIGE'S TIP: If you're on the petite or shorter side, pair these with a high platform shoe to add height. This is a great classic look on just about anybody.

● **Loose-fitting pants in thinner fabrics:** Linen and poplin pants that aren't tapered at the bottom look best on your leg type.

● **Jackets and blouses with structured, padded, or slightly puffed shoulders:** These help create balance between your upper and lower body.

If you feel your thighs are fuller than average, *don't* wear:

● **Skirts with bold prints or in heavy fabrics:** Wearing these types of skirts just draws more attention to your thighs. Avoid large-wale corduroys, velvets, wools, and thicker tweeds, which only add bulk.

Figure 8.2.
The larger knee openings
balance out the thighs.

● **Tight bicycle shorts:** Bicycle shorts that barely cover your thighs have a tendency to ride up, revealing the widest part of your thigh.

● **Pants that taper at the ankle:** The narrow bottoms of these pants accentuate your thighs. If you like the slimmer look, opt for a straight-leg pant.

● **Snug pants:** Pants that are too tight, especially white and light-colored pants, create an effect on your legs that simply is not flattering.

PAIGE'S TIP: Just because a pair of pants fits at the waist, doesn't mean it fits. It's better to find pants that look good through your thighs and legs and then wear a belt or have the waist taken in, instead of jamming your legs into tight pants.

- **Jackets or shirts that stop at the fullest part of your thigh:** Opt for tops that hit slightly below or above the widest part of your thigh.

- **Narrow, clingy skirts:** Skirts that are too narrow around the knee (e.g., a tight pencil skirt) make your thighs look and feel larger.

- **Banded sweaters:** Bulky sweaters with banding around the bottom that hits at the hip draw attention directly to the thigh area.

- **Pants with long pockets:** Front or back pockets that are too long make your thighs the focal point because of the extra detailing around the middle of your legs.

- **Pants or skirts with a vertical stripe or a pintuck:** Tighter bottoms with narrow stripes or a pintuck running up the center of the leg reveal a larger thigh because the lines curve at the thighs instead of running straight up and down.

> **PAIGE SAYS:** A pintuck is when the fabric of a garment is folded and stitched down parallel to the fold. A pintuck is usually an eighth-inch wide, just enough to show the stitches.

If you feel your thighs are too narrow or boyish, *do* wear:

- **Miniskirts:** A-line minis or minis in light colors, prints, or heavier fabrics add dimension to the thighs.

- **Loose-fitting pants in substantial fabrics:** The extra thickness of the fabric helps create more curves.

- **Long sweaters:** Long, bulky sweaters that hit mid-thigh (e.g., cardigans) are a great way to pump up the volume.

- **Pants in lighter colors:** Lighter pants, especially white jeans with a straight or skinny leg, look great on this leg type.

- **Pants with vertical stripes:** If you love pinstripes, opt for a wider stripe or a wider space between the stripes because it gives you the illusion of volume.

- **Pencil skirts:** The sexy shape of this skirt, which tapers at the knee, helps create curves in all the right places.

- **Jackets that hit mid-thigh:** These look great on narrower thighs, especially if there are points of interest around the bottom, such as safari jacket pockets or ruffles. The details at the bottom add thickness and create more dimension.

- **Front pockets:** Pants and skirts that have long front pockets, such as cargo pants, add shape to the thigh area.

If you feel you have narrower or boyish thighs, *don't* wear:

- **Tight flared pants:** Pants that are tight in the hip and thigh area and flared at the bottom distort your body's balance and make your thighs look disproportionately narrow.

- **Pants in thin fabrics:** Fitted pants in really thin fabrications just make your legs look skinnier.

- **Pants that are overly baggy:** Baggy pants, such as loose drawstring pants, can overwhelm your body and make you look lost in your trousers.

- **Anything boxy or broad across the shoulders:** Too much attention to the width of the upper part of your body makes your legs look even thinner.

- **Dark, form-fitting pants without pockets or details:** A darker color with a lack of detail makes your lower half look shapeless and insignificant.

- **Straight, tight miniskirts:** The goal is to add volume, and these skirts do just the opposite. Stick to fuller shapes with added detail to create an area of interest.

- **Overly chunky boots or shoes:** Too much width on the bottom half of your legs makes your upper thighs look too skinny in comparison.

Who Wears Short Shorts?

Finding the right pair of shorts for your body can do wonders for your thighs.

- **Cuffs:** If you have fuller thighs, stay away from cuffs. Cuffs are better for adding volume to leaner thighs. If you're more petite, higher-rise shorts make your legs look longer. If you have longer legs, wear lower-rise shorts.

- **Design:** If you have fuller thighs, stick to clean styles without a lot of detail, especially elaborate front-pocket embellishment. Wear trouser-front or five-pocket-style shorts. If you have leaner thighs, wear cargo shorts or shorts with pocket details around the thighs to add more volume to your upper legs.

- **Color:** If you have fuller thighs, opt for darker solid colors, which make you look leaner. But remember, darker doesn't just mean black! Look for browns, navies, and deeper shades of your favorite colors. For narrower thighs, go for lighter colors. Have fun with whites, light khakis, and brighter shades.

DRESSING IN PROPORTION

The key to really making your thighs look fantastic is to dress right for your whole body. The length of your legs and torso should also dictate your fashion choices. These tips are useful no matter what the size of your thighs.

If you think you have short legs and a long torso, *do* wear:

- **Higher rises:** Pants and skirts with classic to higher rises lengthen your lower body.

- **Tucked-in tops:** Wearing shirts, blouses, and sweaters tucked into your bottom garment helps shorten the torso and elongate the legs.

- **Vertical stripes:** Striped patterns or corduroy fabric on your lower body draws the eye from top to bottom and lengthens the appearance of your legs.

- **Skirts:** Straight or A-line skirts that hit above the knee (even a miniskirt), help elongate the legs, especially if the skirts have a classic to high rise.

PAIGE'S TIP: When wearing skirts that are knee-length and lower, make sure to wear high-heeled boots in the same color; the monochromatic look adds length and is a nice alternative to pants.

- **High-waisted shorts:** Shorts that have an inseam of four to six inches make your legs look longer.

- **Wide-legged pants:** Pants that are wide-legged or slightly flared look great on you because the progressively wider silhouette gives the illusion of having more leg length.

PAIGE'S TIP: Pair these with a nice high-heel or platform shoe for maximum effect.

- **Belts:** Belts of the same color as the other lower-body threads you're wearing make your legs look longer.

If you think you have short legs and a long torso, *don't* wear:

- **Longer tops:** Jackets, blouses, sweaters, or tunics that are too long will dwarf your legs. They'll barely peek out of the bottom.

- **Low-rise capris:** The lower waist and shorter cuffs of these pants only make your legs seem more compact. If you do wear capris, make sure to wear a higher heel with an open toe for added height.

- **Belts slung across your hips:** They draw attention to only the length of your torso and not your legs.

- **Puffy or ruffled skirts:** Too much action below the waistline only emphasizes your shorter bottom half.

- **Drop-waist garments:** Your upper body only appears longer and your lower body shorter when you sport this style.

PAIGE SAYS: A drop waist has a waistline that hits below the natural waistline.

If you think you have long legs and a short torso, *do* wear:

- **Longer sweaters and tops:** The best length for you is at or below the fullest part of your hips. These look especially good with slim-cut jeans or pants.

PAIGE'S TIP: If you think your legs are too long for your body, play up your neckline by wearing interesting collars or neck shapes that spotlight your neck and face.

- **Skirts that fall at or below the knee:** Skirts this length, particularly lower-rise skirts, even out your upper and lower body—and can be very sexy.

- **Dropped waistlines:** Blouses or skirts with dropped waistlines make your upper torso appear longer by drawing the eye down.

- **Pants in many different lengths:** You can wear pants of any length from the knee down, such as pedal pushers, crops, gauchos, and ankle-length pants, but make sure you reach for classic or low rises.

PAIGE SAYS: ⊳ Gauchos are wide-legged cropped pants that hit mid-calf inspired by the South American cowboys called gauchos (Figure 8.3).

- **Cuffs:** Usually cuffs are a no-no, because they can make you look shorter, but if you have longer legs, go for it! Shorts, crops, or pants all look great with cuffs.

Figure 8.3.
Wear low-rise gauchos
for the best look.

If you think you have long legs and a short torso, *don't* wear:

- **High-waisted garments:** Pants, jeans, or skirts with high waists accentuate your shorter upper body. To counteract this, leave your shirts and sweaters untucked to lengthen your look.

- **Monochromatic belts:** Don't wear belts in the same color as your bottom garment or you'll still end up looking like you have a higher waist and shorter torso. Try slinging the belt around your hips to lower the appearance of your waistline.

- **Shorter tops:** Short sweaters, blouses, tops, or vests only cut your upper body in half. The goal is to elongate the upper body instead.

TONING YOUR THIGHS

The thigh area is made up of several major muscle groups: the adductors (your inner thighs), abductors (outer thighs), quadriceps, hamstrings, and glutes. Building stronger thigh muscles involves working all these muscles from your hips to your knees.

To sculpt your thighs, it's important not only to use weight to strengthen the muscles but also to do "stretch and fire" moves to prevent the muscles from getting tight and knotted up. Many people who only lift and neglect to stretch out their muscles complain about the same thing: their legs feel like swollen sausages. When you lift weights, you have lactic acid buildup. By doing an active stretch, you open up the muscle.

To get fabulously toned inner thighs, lifting heavier and heavier weights is not the answer. You can do weighted inner-thigh squeezes until the cows come home, but you'll overtrain the area and build, rather than tone, the muscle. (Try not to increase the weight unless the movement is so easy that it doesn't

GYM DIVAS

Falling into the trap of thinking that you need your body to look great *before* you go to the gym defeats the whole purpose. The weight room is *not* the red carpet. Working out isn't about comparing yourself to anyone else. If you keep making excuses not to go, ask yourself what you're afraid of:

Being alone? Go with a friend.

No gym membership? Ask for a week's pass.

Don't know how to use the machines? Ask for help from the trainers.

Don't feel you have the right clothes to wear? Wear clothes you feel comfortable exercising in, not big, baggy clothes. Wearing clothes that let you see the muscles you're working not only helps you with your form, but also with your confidence. Just do it!

feel like a challenge.) If you have thirty minutes to work on your thighs, you should strengthen and stretch them. Alternate each strength move with an active stretch. Don't skip any steps: shortcuts don't always lead to the right place.

If the moves get too easy, change your foundation. Stand on a Bosu ball or balance on a yoga block. When you change your foundation, you work harder, sweat more, and increase your metabolism.

Finally, the most important thing to keep in mind when working out and stretching your thighs is your foot placement. Where your feet are placed dictates the angles and movement of the rest of your body, so pay attention to your feet when doing any movement. If you decide to use inner- and outer-thigh machines, always ask yourself, "What are my feet doing? Where are my heels?" Follow the instructions in this section's moves to make sure you're firmly grounded.

You'll need:

- A yoga or gym mat
- A foam roller (approximately 3 feet by 4 inches, available at relaxtheback.com)
- A small, weighted ball (1,000 grams/2.2 pounds, 5-inch diameter, like Fitball's Heavymed ball, available at performbetter.com or power-systems.com)

ASHLEY'S TIP: If you can't find or don't have a small, weighted ball, use a folded-up towel or a soccer or kick ball to stabilize yourself in the following moves.

Training Guidelines

1. Do all of the following eight moves in the order provided:
   - Boyfriend roll
   - Lying-down frog stretch and squeeze
   - Lying-down inner-thigh lift
   - Jane Fonda with inner-thigh squeeze
   - Forearm doggie pee
   - Plank with step-throughs
   - The good morning
   - Kick stretch

2. Repeat these moves two to three times, back-to-back.
3. Do this workout two to three times a week.

ASHLEY'S TIP: Do the hips series first to warm up the area. (See Chapter 7.)

The Moves

Follow these expert moves and get fabulously toned thighs.

Boyfriend Roll -

1. Lie down on your tummy. Bring a foam roller next to your lower body with the top slightly angled away from your right hip.
2. Throw your right leg over the roller like you're throwing it over your boyfriend's leg (Figure 8.4). Come up onto your forearms so the pressure is on your inner thighs. Pull your belly button in.
3. Roll back and forth slowly from the very top of your inner thigh to right before your knee. When you hit a knot as you roll, hold and then bend and extend your leg. Repeat for 2 minutes on each leg.

Figure 8.4.
Throw your leg over the roller
as if it is your boyfriend's leg.

Lying-Down Frog Stretch and Squeeze ------------------

1. Lie down on your back with your feet pulled up toward your belly button and the bottoms of your feet touching (Figure 8.5). Inhale deeply.
2. As you exhale, squeeze your pelvic floor and your glutes. Tuck your pubic bone in toward your belly button. Simultaneously, press the bottom edges of your feet together.
3. Hold for 10 seconds, and repeat 5 times.

Figure 8.5.
Inhale and exhale as
you do this stretch.

Lying-Down Inner-Thigh Lift ------------------------------

1. Lie down on your side with your bottom arm underneath you and your shoulder under your ear. Extend your legs straight out under you. You should be able to see your toes. Keep your hips stacked.
2. Bend the knee of your top leg, and place your top foot in front of you at mid-thigh or lower (Figure 8.6). When you look down at your bottom, extended leg, its flexed foot should be parallel to the floor. Hold onto your front leg with your top arm for balance.

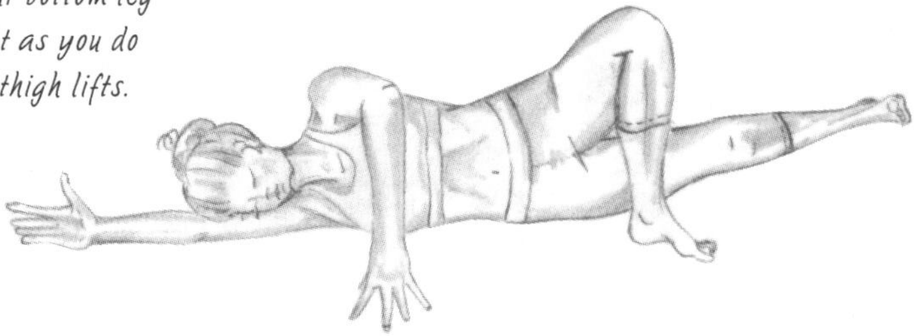

Figure 8.6.
*Keep your bottom leg
straight as you do
inner-thigh lifts.*

3. Push through the heel of your bottom leg with your foot flexed, and fire your inner thigh. Lift your bottom leg off the ground, and do a small lift. Do not let your waistline drop when lifting your top leg. Repeat 20 times. Alternate sides, and repeat 20 times.

ASHLEY'S TIP: Make sure your bottom leg stays straight, and keep the bottom part of your waist lifted off the ground.

Jane Fonda with Inner-Thigh Squeeze - - - - - - - - - - - - - - - - - -

1. Lie down on your back. Bend your knees with your feet flat on the floor. Your knees and feet are hip-width apart. Your arms are spread apart at shoulder height, elbows slightly bent, with the backs of your hands resting on the ground, palms facing up.
2. Place a small weighted ball between your knees. Pull your belly button in, squeeze your glutes, and push your hips up to a bridge position (Figure 8.7).

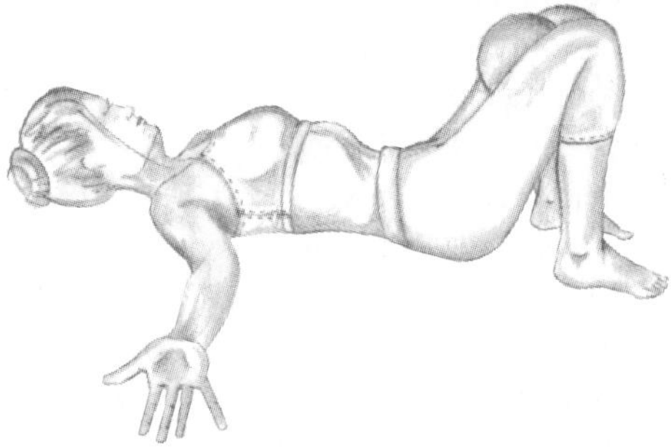

3. Hold and squeeze the ball 20 times, keeping your belly button pulled in. Release back down. Repeat 3 times.

 **ASHLEY'S TIP:**

To make this more challenging, put your feet on stability disks.

Figure 8.7.
Raise your hips while
squeezing a weighted ball.

Forearm Doggie Pee

1. Start on all fours with your upper body resting on your forearms. Your knees are hip-width apart and your belly button is in.

2. Raise one knee up to the side as if you're a dog peeing on a fire hydrant, keeping your foot flexed in line with your knee, both shoulders blocked down, and your eyes facing the ground (Figure 8.8). Bring your knee up as high as possible without rotating your body.

Figure 8.8.
A challenging
version of
forearm doggie
pee should
look like this.

3. Bring your leg back down. Repeat 20 times. Change legs, and repeat another 20 times.

ASHLEY'S TIP: To make this more challenging, start on all fours (in a quadruped position) instead of on your forearms. Use 2-pound ankle weights to make it extra tough.

Plank with Step-Throughs

1. Start in the plank position with your glutes tight, your wrists in line with your shoulders, and your eyes facedown (Figure 8.9).
2. Step your left foot forward as far as possible toward the outside pinky of your left hand and with your toe pointed forward. Keep your left palm glued to the floor, and aim your elbow toward the wall behind you, bending it slightly.
3. Squeeze your right glute, and simultaneously push back through your right heel. Hold for a beat. Change feet. Repeat 10 times.

Figure 8.9.
Follow this form for plank with step-through.

ASHLEY'S TIP: To make this more challenging, add a push-up in between each step-through.

The Good Morning

1. Start in athletic stance, and set your spine. Inter-lace your hands on your tummy, with your knees slightly bent. Bend your torso forward so your back is parallel with the ground (Figure 8.10). Hold for a beat.
2. Push your knees out slightly to the side. Keep your weight in the back of your heels between your first and second toes. Note: if you can't feel the stretch in your hamstrings, your knees may be bent too much. Try straightening out your knees so they are only *slightly* bent.
3. To come up, drive down through your heels and squeeze your glutes. Simultaneously raise your chest up to the ceiling.

ASHLEY'S TIP:

To make this more chal-lenging, interlace your hands behind your head instead of at your tummy.

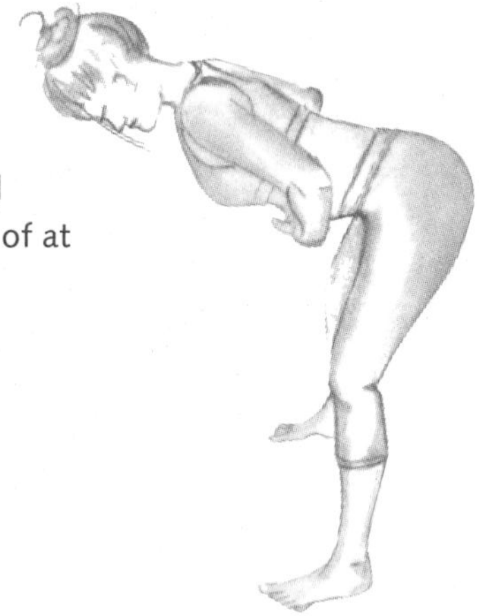

Figure 8.10. Don't lock your knees in the good morning.

Kick Stretch

1. Start with your right foot forward and left foot back behind you as if you're about to take a big step. Flex your back left foot, and pull back with your pinky toe. Move your left arm up in front of

you at eye level, with your palm in and your right arm behind
you. Keep your sternum lifted, your eyes on the horizon, and your
belly button in.

2. With momentum, swing your left foot through and kick it in front
   of you like a Rockette (Figure 8.11). Simultaneously fire (contract)
   the glute of your right leg, switching arms.

3. Bring the right leg back down behind you. Repeat 10 times. Switch
   legs and repeat 10 times.

ASHLEY'S TIP: Don't let your body collapse when kicking.
As you kick, watch the top of your head to make sure you are not
slouching while kicking.

Figure 8.11.
Pull back your pinky toe
when kicking your foot out.

BYE-BYE, THIGHS

Dressing right, eating right, and toning can make those taunts of "thunder thighs" or "string-bean legs" a thing of the past. Focus on strengthening and stretching your muscles and wearing the right outfits for your body shape. Your mood will soar sky high.

Calves and Have Nots

9

Your Ticket to All-Star Calves

*O*nce upon a time, women used to adorn their ankles with jewelry to accentuate their sensuous forms. Now we've got stilettos. How we show off our womanly lower legs can give us style, grace, and elegance. Think Audrey Hepburn with her cropped pants and slender ankles. Wearing different skirts, pants, boots, and shoes can accentuate the thickness and thinness of our calves and balance out our bodies. Plus, what's more fun than shoe shopping? It's a woman's favorite pastime. When we're feeling down, nothing feels as good as a brand-new pair of heels. But make sure that your emotional spending goes to the shoes that are best for you. Find the right fit for your body type, and get ready to flaunt your calves!

CALF ACTION

If you feel you have skinny calves, *do* wear:

- **Straight skirts:** Pencil or straight skirts that hit below the knee or mid-calf show off your slender calves and ankles.

- **Shorts and pants that hit mid-thigh to ankle:** You can get away with wearing all lengths of pants from narrow Bermuda shorts and knickers to straight-leg crops. Your calves look great no matter what!

- **Skinny jeans or pants:** Skinny, tapered, or peg-legged bottoms look great with your skinny calves as long as you balance out your outfit from top to bottom.

If you feel you have skinny calves, *don't* wear:

- **Wide-opening knee-length skirts:** Skirts with too wide a bottom make your calves look like matchsticks.

- **Crops or gauchos:** Shorter pants with leg openings that are too wide give the impression that you're walking on stilts.

- **Very short shorts or miniskirts:** You don't want to show too much leg, or your narrow calves overwhelm your frame.

If you feel you have fuller calves, *do* wear:

- **Knee-length loose shorts or Bermudas:** These longer shorts allow you to show off the smallest part of your leg and even out your proportions, making your calves look smaller. By showing off a little bit above and below the knee, you'll even out your lower legs most efficiently.

- **A-line skirts and dresses:** The wider opening at the bottom of these garments make your calves look leaner.

- **Straight-leg pants:** Pants with nice, straight stovepipe legs or a boot cut or flare mask the size of your calves.

PAIGE SAYS: A stovepipe leg falls straight from the thighs and is wider from the knees down to the floor, with the same-size knee and leg openings (Figure 9.1). The extra fabric won't cling to your calves, making them less noticeable.

Figure 9.1.
Stovepipe pant legs.

- **Cropped pants:** Shorter pants that aren't too skinny in the leg opening are perfect for fuller calves. Gauchos that hit below the calf are your best bet because they allow your ankles to peek out while your calves remain covered.

- **Leggings:** Leggings that stop right where the calf starts to narrow are particularly slimming, especially if the leggings are dark. Shorter leggings only cling to the larger parts of your calf and highlight their size.

- **Skinny jeans:** Find longer skinnies that bunch up around your ankles. These won't cling to your calves, and the extra width around the ankle balances out your calf with the rest of your leg.

If you feel you have fuller calves, *don't* wear:

- **Tapered pants:** Pants that are too tight at the bottom, like super skinny jeans or pants with tapered legs, only cling to your calves.

- **Clingy dresses or skirts that hit mid-calf:** The tight composition and length of these items just draw attention to places you're trying to avoid.

- **Knickers that hit above the calf:** You can wear shorts that end just above the knee, but if you wear knickers that end below the knee and above the calf your leg will have a tubelike appearance.

CINDERELLA STORY: FINDING THE RIGHT SHOES AND BOOTS FOR YOU

No matter how emotional shopping for everyday clothes can be, with the ever-changing shapes and sizes, shoe shopping never ever disappoints. How wonderful that the sizes never seem to change even if you did enjoy a lavish meal the night before! Shoes and boots can work wonders in re-creating an outfit and giving it more style and individuality. They can even balance out your whole body. Finding the perfect shoe for you can make you feel like a fairy princess, so hop in that carriage and get ready to find your very own glass slipper.

If you think you have skinny calves, *do* wear:

- **Pointy-toed shoes:** Delicate shoes that are pointy in the toe add shape to your legs, especially if they're styled to continue the line of your body.

- **Ankle straps:** Shoes with dainty ankle straps draw attention to your lean legs.

- **Stiletto slides:** These sexy woman's shoes that are pointy at the tip with a long, narrow heel of usually three to five inches in height rock for all calf types (Figure 9.2). The narrow band of the slide makes your legs look lean and long. *Wedges* are also universally flattering.

PAIGE SAYS: A wedge is a shoe with a solid one-piece heel. The sole is usually raised slightly and angled upward. The front of the shoe is slightly raised on a platform, which gets higher toward the back of the shoe.

Figure 9.2.
These look great on
all calf types.

- **Lace-up boots:** The laces add bulk to your calves while the cinching in of the laces acts like a corset and gives you that second-skin look, accentuating your calves.

- **Chunky boots:** Combat or motorcycle boots amplify your calves and show off your slender legs. If your calves are extra narrow, opt for a motorcycle boot with a narrower leg opening (so you don't look like you're wearing your father's boots).

- **Skinny jeans tucked into boots:** You may have a difficult time finding boots that fit as snugly as you'd like them to. Find the best possible pair, and then tuck your jeans or pants into them to fill them out. Textured tights or layered socks that peek out the top of your boots also help create fullness.

PAIGE'S TIP: When you're trying to get your skinny jeans into your boots, fold up your pants and put a nylon sock over them. The boots slide right over. Or wrap a rubber band around the bottom of your jeans to hold them down. This works better than stirrups and helps even out your proportions if your thighs are full or you're more carrot-shaped on the bottom.

If you have skinny calves, *don't* wear:

• **Chunky heels, pumps, or sandals:** The thicker base makes your calves look too lean. The less ample the leg, the less ample the heel should be.

• **Clogs:** These Dutch sensations are too heavy for your slender calves and ankles.

• **Mules:** Mules (slip-on shoes with no back, can be open or closed toe) that almost come up to your ankles, as if the shoe was chopped off right before becoming a boot, should have been banned a long time ago. They don't look good on anybody, especially those with leaner limbs.

• **Sock boots:** Boots that look like moccasins with leather on the bottom only make your calves look super skinny instead of shapely.

• **Microfiber boots:** These pull-on boots make you look like you're just wearing tights with heels, especially when you wear them in dark colors.

If you think you have fuller calves, *do* wear:

• **Sculpted heels:** Heels with form, such as espadrilles or wedges, beautify your fuller calves by shaping your lower legs.

• **Flip-flops and thongs:** These summertime basics work wonders at taking the eye away from your calf and down toward your toes. A great pedicure or cute toe-ring can help, too!

• **Chunkier heels:** Thicker calves look best in chunky shoes. The more ample the calf, the more ample the heel should be. It's simply a matter of balance—literally!

• **Clogs:** Wooden clogs of any height look great on you because the heaviness of the shoe creates balance with the calf.

• **Semi-structured boots:** Enjoy wearing fun, winter-style boots that are semi-structured, such as Uggs and moccasin boots. The bulkier nature of this type of boot masks what's underneath

Figure 9.3.
These boots hide
what's underneath.

while keeping you nice and toasty (Figure 9.3).

• **Pull-up or zip-up knee-length boots:** The higher the boots hit, the more they draw out the calves and mask any unwanted thickness and volume.

• **Wedge-heel boots:** Shapely heels on boots look best on you, making the bottom part of your leg appear more sculpted.

If you think you have fuller calves, *don't* wear:

• **Ankle straps:** Shoes with ankle straps aren't the most flattering for your leg type, because the strap acts like a shelf with your calves on display.

• **Stiletto heels:** Stay away from too tiny a stiletto heel, because your calves overpower your shoes.

• **Pointy-toed flats:** The narrower the toe, the more compact your calf looks.

• **Kitten heels:** These baby heels are just too dainty for your calves.

> **PAIGE SAYS:** Kitten heels are a woman's shoe with a short, slender heel, usually one and a half to two inches high with a slight curve. The style was popularized by Audrey Hepburn. They are particularly common on sandals.

• **Slouchy, unstructured boots:** Boots like this, especially ones that hit mid-calf, only draw excess attention to your calves by severing the line of your leg and bulking you up where you need it the least.

• **Tight, tubular boots:** Don't squeeze your calves into too tight a boot. If the ankle or calf of the boot is overly snug, your calf looks even larger. Tubular boots without shape will cut off your circulation and leave you with unsightly and uncomfortable bands around the tops of your legs.

THESE BOOTS WERE MADE FOR WALKING

*T*o find the best pair of boots for your calves, measure the circumference of your calves at their fullest point. Then call stores and ask how narrow or full their boots really are. Many websites specialize in boots with different circumferences: there are actually over twenty different widths to choose from. If worse comes to worst, call your local shoe doctor. He or she can take in or stretch out boots and can even insert a gusset to create more width. Boots are particularly great if your ankles and calves lack definition; so are dark, textured stockings with patterns and lace.

If you think you have shorter legs, *do* wear:

• **Slingback high heels:** These help lengthen the look of your legs since they don't have any straps to bisect the line of your foot. These smashing heels are especially flattering in skin and neutral colors.

• **D'Orsay pumps:** These flattering pumps are very sexy. The vamp of the shoe (i.e., the front part of the shoe that covers your toes and your instep) is cut away very close to the toe box, and the sides of the shoe are also cut away (Figure 9.4). Toe cleavage actually lengthens your legs and looks great on shorter legs.

• **Stiletto slides:** These lengthen the leg because of their shallow coverage.

• **Really high platform boots or shoes:** Your legs look a mile long in high-heeled platforms. Plus, platforms are probably the most comfortable shoes to wear since you're not teetering around on them.

Figure 9.4.
These pumps work wonders on shorter legs.

If you think you have shorter legs, *don't* wear:

• **High mules:** These mules come up near your ankles and sever your legs in the wrong places, shortening their look.

• **Ankle straps:** These straps chop up shorter legs, emphasizing their shorter length.

• **Kitten heels:** Go for height instead of a tiny heel! The higher, the better.

• **Superhigh boots:** Boots that come up over your knees make you look like you're all boot. You'll wonder where your legs went.

• **Square-toed boots or shoes:** The abrupt toe ending makes your feet and legs look too compact.

If you think you have longer legs, *do* wear:

• **Kitten heels:** Sexy little kitten heels are fun and easy to walk in. Experiment with different styles and colors.

• **Ballet flats:** Flats look great on you since you already have height naturally. And it's good for your body to take a break from high heels.

• **Ankle straps:** Because your leg is long, you can get away with the strap breaking up your leg.

• **Mary Janes:** You're the only leg type who can get away with wearing these retro, sassy shoes, especially with short skirts or cropped pants—so go for it!

If you feel you have longer legs, *don't* wear:

• **Ankle boots:** These short boots make your legs look out of proportion. If you have really long legs and like to wear short skirts or cropped pants, ankle boots definitely aren't the right choice for you.

• **Really high platforms or boots:** Stay away from superhigh platforms unless you can balance out your upper half with the lower half of your body.

FITNESS FOR YOUR CALVES

Sometimes we don't think about our calves until we don a new pair of heels and wonder why our calves don't look fabulous. How could they when we neglect them so much? We use our calves throughout the day without even thinking about it, but when it comes time for the gym, it's the last body part we want to work on. Plus there's the looming myth that if we work out our calves, they'll get big and bulky. No! The exact opposite is true.

To shape your calves, you *have* to strengthen and stretch them. When your calves aren't strong, they tend to look flabby and shapeless. Many women know that muscle weighs more than fat. What that really means is that muscle takes up less space and volume in your body. If you convert your fat to muscle by working out, there will be less mass, which means less you! If you held up ten pounds of fat next to ten pounds of muscle, you would see how much less space the muscle takes up. By strengthening your calves, they'll actually *look* smaller. When you *don't* work out your calves, they get tight and cause other problems, such as hip and lower-back pain and cramping.

Yes, it is true that having thin or full calves is partly genetic. But what you do to them makes all the difference. If you're blessed with large calves with some muscle, you can whittle them down to shapely legs, even if you feel like they resemble tree trunks. If you start with skinny calves, you can build them up from nothing and help balance out the shape of your lower body. Even "carrot stick" or "drumstick" legs (i.e., when the leg is disproportionately thicker on top and skinnier on the bottom) can be improved. Working out your calves can make your whole lower body look better. And you don't need a fancy calf machine to accomplish this.

Walk the Walk

How you walk partly determines the shape of your calves and legs, so be sure to use proper form. What's the perfect stride?

1. Step forward.
2. Land on your heel.

3. Roll through your foot.
4. Push off between your first and second toe.

But what about when you power walk at different inclines?

On a Flat Surface

1. Keep your arms close to your sides.
2. Pull your arms back with your elbows as you walk.
3. Keep your sternum lifted and your eyes on the horizon.

Uphill

1. Cross your arms in front of you.
2. Pull your arms back with your elbows.

Downhill

1. Keep your weight in the back of your heels and glutes.
2. Don't support yourself by your kneecaps.

On a Treadmill

1. Keep your eyes on the horizon.
2. If the TV at the gym is very high up and requires you to strain your neck to see it, listen to music or a book on CD and focus on your breathing instead.

Working Your Calves

You'll need:

- A PVC pipe (3 feet by 4 inches, available at Home Depot or select hardware stores) or a foam roller
- A yoga or gym mat

Training Guidelines

1. Do all of the following five moves in the order provided:
   - Calf roll-outs
   - Alternating active heel stretch
   - Wide-sumo-squat heel lifts
   - One-twos
   - Downward dog with active heel press

2. Repeat the series two to three times, back-to-back.

3. Do this workout two to three times a week.

ASHLEY'S TIP:  Do the hips series first to warm up the area. (See Chapter 7.)

The Moves

These moves will help strengthen and tone those oft-neglected calves.

Calf Roll-Outs -

1. Lie down on your back. Place the PVC pipe under your Achilles tendon (i.e., the backs of your ankles), and cross your right ankle over your left ankle, with your hands behind your head (Figure 9.5).

2. Leading with your big toe and keeping your feet flexed, slowly rotate your legs from side to side on top of the PVC pipe. If you feel like you've hit a knot, rotate the ankle of the bottom foot two times in each direction. Repeat rolling back and forth for 1 minute.

3. Then slide the PVC pipe up to the centers of your calves. Repeat the movement, rotating your legs from side to side for another minute.

ASHLEY'S TIP: Rolling out is important because it massages the calves, deeply loosening any knots in your muscles and preventing awful late-night calf cramps.

Figure 9.5.
Rotate legs from side to side
to roll out your calves.

Alternating Active Heel Stretch ----------------------

1. Stand with your heels off the edge of a stable surface approximately 1 foot off the ground. A treadmill or step is a good option. Hold onto the wall in front of you for balance.
2. Move your right foot forward several inches, and slightly bend the right knee. Place the ball of your left foot on the edge of the surface, and drive your left heel straight down to the ground (Figure 9.6). Try to push down through the *outside* edge of the heel, squeezing the left glute as you push the heel down. Keep your eyes on the horizon, and hold your belly button in.
3. Pushing through your toes, raise your left heel up as high as you can (or "relevé up"), pushing the right heel down. Repeat 12 times, alternating feet.

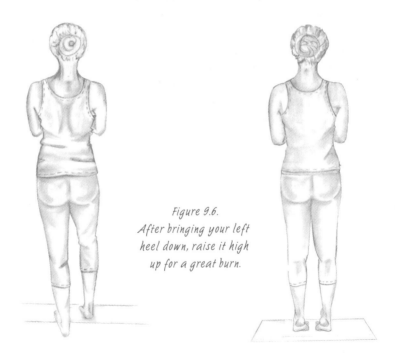

Figure 9.6.
After bringing your left
heel down, raise it high
up for a great burn.

ASHLEY'S TIP: After you've been walking in high heels (which shortens your calf and Achilles tendon), make sure to stretch out your calves. If you don't, they'll become tight, little angry balls.

Wide-Sumo-Squat Heel Lifts ------------------------------

1. Stand with your feet slightly
   wider than athletic stance
   and slightly turned out.
   Set your spine.
2. Bend your knees into a
   deep squat. Sit back into
   your glutes with your
   elbows resting on top of
   your knees. Keep your
   belly button in and your
   eyes on the ground.
3. From the wide-squat position, raise one heel up, or
   relevé up. Lower it down
   to the ground. Alternate
   right and left heels, and
   repeat 10 times.

Figure 9.7.
To make this more challenging, interlace
your hands behind your head.

ASHLEY'S TIP: To
make this more challenging, interlace your hands behind your
head (Figure 9.7) while squatting, keeping your elbows pushing outward. Make sure your head is in line with your spine. You
should feel this move in your quads, glutes, *and* calves.

One-Twos ---

1. Stand on the edge of a treadmill or stable surface approximately
   1 foot off the floor, holding onto the wall in front of you for balance (Figure 9.8).
2. Take one foot and wrap it around the back of your other ankle.
   Drive the standing heel straight down with your glutes tight.
3. Raise your standing heel back up, or relevé up, so it's parallel with
   the ground, counting "One." Pause. Then raise the heel even
   higher, counting "Two." Pause. Drive the heel back down again.
4. Repeat 5 times with the standing foot straight. Repeat 5 times
   with the standing foot turned out. Repeat 5 times with the stand-

ing foot pigeon-toed. Repeat the entire series standing on the opposite foot.

ASHLEY'S TIP: To make this more challenging, hold an 8- to 15-pound weight in one hand.

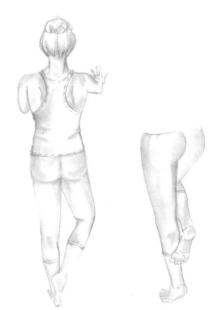

Figure 9.8.
Wrap one foot around
your ankle, and lift up.

Downward Dog with Active Heel Press

1. Start on the ground on all fours. Lift your knees slightly off the ground, and push back into a downward dog (a common yoga pose in which the body forms a triangle with the weight distributed between the arms and legs) with your knees slightly bent and your hands pushing the floor away. Adjust your hands

so they're just wider than shoulder-width apart and your feet so they're just wider than hip-width apart (Figure 9.9).

2. Keeping your eyes on your belly button, alternate driving one heel down to the ground at a time, squeezing the glute of the foot that's driving down. Alternate 10 times.
3. Walk your feet to your hands. Bring in your feet hip-width apart. Interlace your hands behind your head with your chin tucked to your throat.
4. Drive down through your heels, and squeeze your glutes, rolling up one vertebra at a time.

*Figure 9.9.
Drive one heel
down at a time.*

OUR TWO CENTS

Remember not to neglect your calves either in the gym or after a long day of standing or walking on unforgiving surfaces. Stretching and strengthening your calves can change their shape and make shoe shopping even more fun. Focusing on the aesthetic *and* strength benefits of toned calves ensures that they look and feel great in any outfit you choose. And you and your calves will live happily ever after.

The S.O.S. Food Plan

10

Setting Your Nutritional Foundation

*N*ow that you've learned how to use fashion and fitness to help you look and feel your best, it's time to focus on how to nourish your well-dressed, newly toned body. Most of us know how to eat when we're on a *diet*, but once we "go off," we're lost.

THE S.O.S. FOOD PLAN PHILOSOPHY

The S.O.S. Food Plan (Satiation of the Senses) isn't another fad: it's a nutritional foundation. The S.O.S. Food Plan provides basic tools that endure over time; it is *not* a quick way to drop seventeen pounds in three days—and then gain it all right back. *Note: always consult your physician before starting a new eating plan.*

The three main characteristics of the S.O.S. Food Plan are as follows:

1. It's simple. There's no incessant weighing and measuring of food.
2. You won't feel hungry or deprived. (Who wants to feel like that all day?)
3. It teaches you to handle your food from a mental and behavioral perspective.

This food plan stems from Ashley's successful experiences in following a food plan while she was in treatment and then working with top nutritionists to cater the plan to active women living lean, livable lifestyles. Ashley has seen the evidence of the plan's success on many fronts, including incredible lifestyle changes, body changes, weight loss, increased mental stability, and overall happiness. You will, too!

S.O.S. = Satiation of the Senses

The key to the S.O.S. Food Plan is to stimulate all five senses when you eat: sight, sound, touch, taste, and smell. With lunch and dinner, you should have something hot, cold, crunchy, and colorful. If your meal contains these four elements, you're much less likely to overeat, because the texture itself is very satiating. Eating a cup of soup, a crunchy salad, and half a turkey sandwich for lunch is actually more satisfying and keeps you feeling fuller for longer than if you scarf down a big bowl of pasta. We tend to overeat some foods, such as pasta, pizza, ice cream, and even Chinese food, because the consistency is so uniform that we don't even know we're full until we're ridiculously bloated and ready for a long nap. The more color and crunch in your meal, the more vitamins, minerals, and fiber you're getting. If your meal has no color, chances are it has few nutrients.

You'll need:

- A small journal or easy-to-carry notebook
- A permanent marker to label your water bottles
- A travel pack cooler (hard or soft) to pack snacks
- Small ice packs for the cooler
- A water container that you like to look at
- An egg timer

THE THREE-STEP PLAN

The S.O.S. Food Plan has three steps:

1. Identify your goals.
2. Journal for eleven days.
3. Follow the eating guidelines.

Step 1: Identify Your Goals

The first step to achieving a solid foundation is to identify your physical, emotional, behavioral, and nutritional goals. You will become your own life coach. To succeed at anything, you must first know what you're trying to achieve. Grab your new journal or use the template in Appendix C, and write one to three specific, realistic goals for each category of what you *will* do. You can update your goals after each week and continually add to them.

• **Physical:** These goals relate to your level of physical activity. For example, "I commit to three forty-five-minute sessions of fat-burning cardio a week for the next two weeks."

PHONE A FRIEND

*H*aving an S.O.S. Food Plan buddy can help both of you achieve your goals. Find a friend, relative, or coworker you trust, and start the plan together.

1. **E-mail each other your goals.** You can also e-mail your food journals to each other for some extra accountability. You don't need a nutritionist on staff to succeed with this plan. As you exchange food records, evaluate your friend's progress based on *her* goals, not yours. This is not a competition.

2. **Find a training buddy.** It's much easier to back out of a workout if you're training by yourself. Make weekly dates with a friend to keep fitness from falling on the back burner. Working out with a friend also makes the whole experience more enjoyable, and fitness is supposed to be fun! Workouts are the new coffee dates.

3. **Try a cooking exchange.** Swap meals with a friend, and alternate nights of cooking. Host a cooking party. If you're not comfortable in the kitchen, but your friend is a gourmet chef, offer to help her with other tasks such as babysitting or closet organizing if she helps with food preparation.

- **Emotional:** These goals relate to how you let (or don't let) your emotions affect your eating. For example, "Instead of stopping at Baskin-Robbins and eating ice cream when I get fed up with work, I'll go home and e-mail a friend."

- **Behavioral:** These goals relate to actions you can take to improve your well-being. For example, "I will prepare my food on Sunday and Wednesday for the upcoming week."

- **Nutritional:** These goals relate to your food intake. For example, "I will eat a fruit with a fat for my two snacks each day."

Step 2: Journal for Eleven Days

Writing down your food and beverage intake along with your accompanying emotions can be a real wake-up call. You don't have to journal for the rest of your life—just track what you eat for the first eleven days on the plan. If you enjoy journaling, by all means, keep at it! The more information you record, the easier it is for you to play detective and begin to understand what your body wants and needs.

Using your journal or the template in Appendix D, record every meal and snack you eat with your accompanying feelings. The "feelings" part of the journal is critical. One of the biggest problems people have is separating their emotions from their food. Write down two to three adjectives describing your feelings before you eat. When you write *frustrated* or *angry*, you release your feelings on paper and not on the food you're about to devour. Most the time we're unconscious about *why* we're eating. Writing down your feelings gives you a moment to stop and think about it.

Also, record how each meal or snack affects you physically. If you suffer from feeling bloated or feeling too hyper and then lethargic during the day, it's important to understand why. You start to realize that maybe that big headache was caused by waiting much too long to eat lunch. You can identify the crime and prevent it from happening next time.

You also become aware of your trigger foods. A trigger food is any food that you can't stop eating until there's nothing left. Cake, cookies, cupcakes, movie popcorn, the bread basket, pizza, and pasta can open up Pandora's box. Start keeping a list of your trigger foods, and avoid them for eleven days.

Finally, record your physical activity. By writing down what you did, how long you did it for, and how vigorous a workout it was (on a scale of 1 to 5), you become more conscious of your activity and can assess your progress as you become more active.

And remember, just because your favorite celebrities are using one eating plan doesn't mean it's right for you. An eating plan should be tailored to your body's individual needs. Slow down, simplify, and check in.

Step 3: Follow the Eating Guidelines

The key to the S.O.S. food plan is being aware of your portion sizes and what you're eating when.

• **Timing:** No matter what, eat every two to three hours. Your body is like a furnace. Keep it fueled!

• **Water:** Drink at least one hundred ounces a day for the first eleven days. Then aim for at least two to three large (thirty-two-ounce) bottles a day.

• **Food:** For the first six days on the plan, your food intake and portions should be as follows:

Breakfast: One portion of carb, one portion of protein, and one portion of fat
Snack: One portion of fat and one portion of fruit
Lunch: One portion of protein, two portions of vegetables, and one portion of carb
Snack: One portion of fat and one portion of fruit
Dinner: One portion of protein, two portions of vegetables, and one portion of starchy vegetable
Snack: One treat: one sugar-free hot chocolate, one sugar-free Popsicle, or one fruit

• **Multivitamin:** Take a multivitamin (newpfc.com). Because this food plan has no dairy, you also need the calcium, but not the lactose, that is in dairy. Be sure to take your multivitamin in the morning with food. Most multivitamins have vitamin B_{12}. B_{12} gives you great energy. If taken too late, it can keep you up at night.

Note: There is no dairy in the plan (see "Frequently Asked Questions" later in this chapter), but if you would like to include it, add one portion of dairy per day instead of a protein. For example, at breakfast, you could have one carb (cereal), one *dairy* (one cup skim milk), and one fat (one tablespoon of peanut butter) instead of one carb, one *protein*, and one fat.

Also, for one special meal during days one through six, you can add either one glass of alcohol, one extra carb, or one special dessert treat that is not on the plan.

On the seventh day of the plan, take the day off. Being hungry or in deprivation mode is no way to lead your life. It ends up flip-flopping, and you'll end up bingeing. It may not happen that week, month, or year, but it'll happen. The trick is to eat cleanly six days a week and then take a day off. On an off day, you don't have to be conscious of your food, how often you eat, your portion sizes, your water intake, or your cardio. Chances are, you'll be more than eager to get back on the plan the next day. If the idea of an off day makes you too nervous, instead have three off meals throughout the course of the week whenever you like.

What's a Portion?

These portions are a good rule of thumb when following the S.O.S. Food Plan.

- Carbs
  Beans: ½ fist size
  Dry cereal: 1 fist size
  Hot cereal: ½ fist size
  Rice: ½ fist size
  Potatoes: 1 fist size
- Dairy
  Cheese (mozzarella, light Jarlsberg, cheddar, Parmesan,
    2 percent string cheese): 1 thin slice
  Greek or low-fat yogurt: 1 fist size
  Low-fat cottage cheese: 1 fist size
  Skim milk: 1 cup
  Soy milk: 1 cup
- Fat
  All-natural almond, cashew, or peanut butter: 1 level tablespoon (Note: don't dump out the oil in the jar—mix it in.)

Avocado: ¼ unit

Nuts (whole nuts such as almonds, cashews, hazelnuts, peanuts): 12 nuts

Oils (olive, sunflower, safflower): 1 tablespoon

Seeds (pumpkin, sesame, sunflower, flaxseed): ⅛ cup

ASHLEY'S TIP: Stir the peanut butter before refrigerating it.

- Fruits

Apples, all berries, grapes, kiwi, oranges, peaches, pears, pineapple, plums, watermelon: 1 fist size or one unit

Banana, grapefruit, papaya, mango, cantaloupe, honeydew melon: ½ unit

Fruit juices: ½ cup

- Protein

Beef: size and thickness of the palm of your hand

Canned tuna in water: 1 cup

Eggs: 2 whole eggs or 5 egg whites

Fish: entire hand width and from wrist to tip of longest finger

Poultry: entire hand width and from wrist to tip of longest finger

Soy: soybean curd or firm tofu: 1 palm size

Soybean milk: 1 cup

- Vegetables

Colorful vegetables: 2 fist sizes

Carb vegetables (peas and corn): 1 fist size

Vegetable soups (preferably homemade): 1 cup

See Appendix E for calorie information and Appendix F for a detailed grocery list.

THE FOOD PLAN: FOURTEEN DAYS

Here are two weeks' worth of meals that follow the S.O.S. guidelines. Using this plan as a baseline, you may customize meals to your tastes. Refer back to the "What's a Portion" section when creating your menu.

Day One

7:00 A.M.   2 scrambled eggs or 5 egg whites; 1 piece of whole-grain toast or low-carb tortilla with salsa; multivitamin; tea, coffee, and/or water with lemon

10:00 A.M.   12 almonds, 1 apple with sprinkle of cinnamon

1:00 P.M.   1 6-ounce can of tuna, rinsed, with ½ bag of spinach leaves, lots of colored veggies, ½ yam, and balsamic vinaigrette

4:00 P.M.   ½ cup of juice, 12 cashews

7:00 P.M.   Grilled chicken breast; small, colorful, crunchy salad with balsamic vinaigrette; steamed broccoli; 1 small ear of corn

10:00 P.M.   1 cup of hot chocolate with nonfat milk

Day Two

7:00 A.M.   1 packet size of oatmeal (add cinnamon and nutmeg) made with soy milk or low-fat milk; multivitamin; tea, coffee, and/or water with lemon

10:00 A.M.   12 cashews, ½ cantaloupe

1:00 P.M.   Grilled turkey breast with mixed greens and lots of colored veggies, ½ baked potato, 1 small bowl of veggie soup

4:00 P.M.   ½ banana with a sprinkle of nutmeg, 1 level tablespoon of natural almond, cashew, or peanut butter

7:00 P.M.   Grilled salmon, salad with balsamic vinaigrette, steamed broccoli

10:00 P.M.   1 sugar-free chocolate ice pop

Day Three

7:00 A.M.   4 to 5 scrambled egg whites with tomato, basil, and a sprinkle of pepper; multivitamin; tea, coffee, and/or water with lemon

10:00 A.M.   12 almonds, 6 strawberries

1:00 P.M.   1 low-carb tortilla; ¼ pound thinly sliced turkey breast with lettuce, tomato, cucumber, and spicy mustard

4:00 P.M.   ½ honeydew melon, 12 almonds

7:00 P.M. Sirloin steak, steamed asparagus, mixed greens with balsamic vinaigrette and lots of colored veggies
10:00 P.M. 1 cup of hot chocolate with soy milk

Day Four

7:00 A.M. Hot oatmeal with 1 scoop of protein powder; multivitamin; tea, coffee, and/or water with lemon
10:00 A.M. 12 cashews, 2 small peaches
1:00 P.M. Grilled chicken breast with mixed greens and lots of colored veggies, ½ baked potato
4:00 P.M. Applesauce and 1 level tablespoon of natural almond or peanut butter
7:00 P.M. Swordfish fillet, salad with balsamic vinaigrette, green beans
10:00 P.M. Handful of mixed berries

Day Five

7:00 A.M. New PFC (whey protein) vanilla shake with a handful of frozen berries; multivitamin; tea, coffee, and/or water with lemon
10:00 A.M. ½ banana and 1 tablespoon of peanut butter
1:00 P.M. Lean ground beef, chicken, or turkey tacos in corn tortilla with ¼ avocado; small salad
4:00 P.M. Handful of strawberries, 12 cashews
7:00 P.M. Chicken breast, snow peas, sliced peppers, and cucumber
10:00 P.M. Sliced apples with cinnamon and 2 tablespoons of wheat germ

Day Six

7:00 A.M. 1 cup of Optimum cereal with nonfat milk, berries, multivitamin
10:00 A.M. Almonds and ½ cup of fresh orange juice
1:00 P.M. 2 fist sizes of colorful salad with greens and veggies and sliced chicken breast and ½ cup of rice
4:00 P.M. 1 apple and 1 tablespoon of peanut butter
7:00 P.M. White fish with asparagus and corn (not creamed)
10:00 P.M. All-fruit ice pop

Day Seven

7:00 A.M. 4-egg-white omelet with cooking spray; ¼ avocado, peppers, and tomatoes; 1 piece of whole-grain toast; multivitamin

10:00 A.M. ½ mango with lime, 12 cashews

1:00 P.M. Tuna fish with mustard, onions and chopped celery on a bed of lettuce, 1 cup of noncanned tomato rice soup

4:00 P.M. 1 orange; 12 almonds

7:00 P.M. Turkey breast, 2 fist sizes of mixed salad greens, ½ artichoke dipped in balsamic vinaigrette

10:00 P.M. Sugar-free chocolate ice pop

Day Eight

7:00 A.M. 2 big squares of shredded wheat with soy milk (heated), applesauce, and 1 tablespoon peanut butter; multivitamin; tea, coffee, and/or water with lemon

10:00 A.M. ½ cantaloupe, sunflower seeds

1:00 P.M. Turkey burger on ½ whole-grain bun with grilled onions, lettuce, and tomato (avocado optional); steamed broccoli

4:00 P.M. Watermelon, 12 walnuts

7:00 P.M. Shrimp stir-fry with snow peas, peppers, onions, and zucchini; steamed edamame with kosher salt

10:00 P.M. Fat-free, sugar-free chocolate pudding

Day Nine

7:00 A.M. 1 hard-boiled egg and 3 hard-boiled egg whites; 1 slice multigrain bread with almond butter; sliced tomatoes; multivitamin; tea, coffee, and/or water with lemon

10:00 A.M. Pineapple, 12 cashews

1:00 P.M. Grilled chicken with tomato, cucumber, mustard, and 1 slice cheese on ½ whole-wheat pita (heated); small mixed green salad

4:00 P.M. 2 clementines, 12 peanuts

7:00 P.M.   Grilled or broiled steak (marinated overnight in teriyaki sauce), topped with sautéed mushrooms and grilled onions; small side salad

ASHLEY'S TIP: Marinating any meat overnight saves calories by locking in flavor without the need for heavy sauces.

10:00 P.M.   Mint tea with honey, lemon, and cayenne pepper

Day Ten

7:00 A.M.   New PFC (whey protein) chocolate shake with 1 tablespoon peanut butter and ½ banana, cinnamon, and nutmeg; multivitamin; tea, coffee, and/or water with lemon

10:00 A.M.   Blueberries with sprinkled sunflower seeds

1:00 P.M.   Chopped salad with turkey, peppers, cucumbers, tomatoes, and carrots with warm brown rice or couscous, and olive oil and balsamic vinegar

4:00 P.M.   Plum, 12 peanuts

7:00 P.M.   Barbeque chicken (marinated in barbeque sauce overnight), corn on the cob (find sweet corn that tastes good without butter, or spray it with no-calorie butter spray and sprinkle with salt), grilled asparagus and baby tomatoes

10:00 P.M.   Cranberry juice frozen ice pop

Day Eleven

7:00 A.M.   Hot oatmeal with nonfat or soy milk, ½ scoop of protein powder, and 1 tablespoon wheat germ; multivitamin; tea, coffee, and/or water with lemon

10:00 A.M.   Pear with 1 tablespoon cashew butter

1:00 P.M.   Egg salad (1 hard-boiled egg, 2 hard-boiled egg whites with mustard, scallions, celery, and red pepper flakes) on 2 Wasa crackers, sliced tomato, celery sticks, low-sodium tomato soup

4:00 P.M.   Sliced mango with avocado and lime juice

7:00 P.M.   Roast turkey with mashed sweet potato and steamed broccoli, low-sodium vegetable soup

10:00 P.M.   Fat-free, sugar-free strawberry gelatin dessert with 1 tablespoon fat-free whipped cream

Day Twelve

7:00 A.M. Greek yogurt with mixed berries, with Fiber One sprinkled on it; multivitamin; tea, coffee, and/or water with lemon

10:00 A.M. ½ cup freshly squeezed orange juice (about 2 oranges), mixed with Udo's Oil

1:00 P.M. Turkey with cucumber and tomato, topped with salsa on a low-carb wrap, heated; raw yellow and red bell pepper strips with hummus

4:00 P.M. Apple with wheat germ and cinnamon

7:00 P.M. Chicken or beef fajitas: strips of meat sautéed with onions, peppers, and spices, topped with salsa and guacamole; small dinner salad

10:00 P.M. Sliced strawberries with 1 tablespoon fat-free fruit-juice-sweetened chocolate syrup, heated (from Wax Orchards)

Day Thirteen

7:00 A.M. 1 piece multigrain toast with 2 scrambled eggs, 1 piece low-fat cheese, and 1 slice of tomato; multivitamin; tea, coffee, and/or water with lemon

10:00 A.M. ½ grapefruit sprinkled with ground flaxseeds

1:00 P.M. Turkey chili, small mixed green salad with olive oil and balsamic vinegar, small whole-grain roll

4:00 P.M. Blackberries and walnuts

7:00 P.M. Grilled salmon; string beans; cucumber, tomato, and onion salad (marinated for at least 2 hours in a mix of balsamic vinegar and water and sprinkled with dill)

10:00 P.M. Fat-free, sugar-free vanilla pudding

Day Fourteen

7:00 A.M. French toast (1 piece multigrain bread dipped in 2 eggs, skim milk, cinnamon, and nutmeg and prepared on skillet sprayed with cooking spray) topped with honey, pure maple syrup, or a whole-fruit spread and slivered almonds; multivitamin; tea, coffee, and/or water with lemon

10:00 A.M. Blueberries sprinkled with sunflower seeds

1:00 P.M. Low-sodium vegetable soup; ½ grilled chicken sandwich with hummus, tomato, and sprouts on multigrain bread
4:00 P.M. Apple with wheat germ and cinnamon
7:00 P.M. Turkey burger wrapped in butter lettuce, topped with tomato, grilled onions, and avocado or low-fat cheese; baked french fries (slice a fist-size potato into wedges, coat lightly with olive oil and kosher salt, and bake at 350 degrees for 35 minutes or until edges are brown, turning once)
10:00 P.M. Hot apple cider with cinnamon stick

FREQUENTLY ASKED QUESTIONS

Where's the dairy? Sometimes when we feel heavy, we're really just bloated, and dairy tends to be extremely bloating. Try going eleven days without having any. The lactose in many dairy products can be a major bloating culprit. Take a calcium supplement to make sure you're getting adequate calcium, and take note of your body's response. Are you less bloated? Are your waistbands less tight? Do you feel better? If so, you may have trouble digesting dairy. If you don't notice any difference and really miss your dairy, add it back slowly. But if cheese is a trigger food, save it for your off day or just eliminate it.

How can I drink all that water? It may seem like a lot to drink 100 ounces of water a day, but keeping dehydration at bay is so important. If you tend to get headaches, constipation, or dry skin, try drinking more water and see if that helps. Here are a few tips:

1. If you just can't stand looking at another water bottle, buy your own personal bottle that has some meaning or is aesthetically pleasing. Keep washing it out and reusing.
2. Take three bottles of water in the morning, and label them with a marker: 1, 2, and 3. Then you'll be able to keep track of your intake all day long. To reuse the same water bottle, mark what number you're on as you go.

3. Give yourself mini-goals throughout the day. Try to drink a certain amount by 9:00 A.M., noon, and 4:00 P.M.

4. Add fresh lemon, cucumber, or herbal tea bags to vary the flavor.

5. Avoid sodas, diet sodas, or any other liquids that hamper your water intake.

6. Try water at room temperature; it tends to go down easier.

You may feel full and bloated when you start drinking a lot of water while you're not used to it. You'll also be urinating more because you're flushing out your system. Don't panic: your body will assimilate. The good news is that when you wake up in the mornings, your tummy will feel flat and your body will be less bloated because you've flushed out your system the day before.

I thought eating carbs and fat would make me *gain* weight. The S.O.S. Food Plan promotes body transformation through smart eating. Eliminating carbs altogether does not make sense. Eating carbohydrates at the beginning of the day and at lunch is important because at those times, you're eating to get fuel, energy, and maximum fat burning. At dinner, you don't need that jolt of carbohydrate-driven energy, because you're usually winding down your day. There are good (i.e., complex) carbs and bad carbs (e.g., white bread). Good carbs keep your blood sugar even and keep you feeling fuller longer because it takes the body longer to process them, whereas bad carbs just fuel the fire as your body quickly breaks the food down into sugar.

Also, if a carbohydrate or any food has partially hydrogenated oil in the list of ingredients, as many breads, pastas, muffins, cereals, or candies do, throw it and run the other way. Partially hydrogenated oil is a manufactured oil used to make products last longer on the shelf, and it is completely unnatural.

ASHLEY'S TIP: In the ingredient list on any food label, the placement of an ingredient shows how much of it the food contains (Figure 10.1). For example, if white flour is listed first on the label, the product is made up of mostly white flour.

Fat is also important for keeping you feeling satisfied. Eliminating fat is certainly not the answer. Nuts, all-natural peanut butter, avocados, or extra-virgin olive oil is vital for your health. Fat is a source of energy. It adds taste and texture to foods, makes us feel fuller for longer, and helps the body absorb fat-soluble vitamins such as vitamins A, D, E, and K.

Why do I need to pair a fruit with fat? When you have a sugar, such as a cup of fruit, you should have a fat with it to balance out the resulting insulin spike. If you're having an apple, add a tablespoon of peanut butter or twelve almonds. You'll feel satisfied and fuller longer. You can maintain the burst of energy over a longer period of time.

If you would prefer to substitute a vegetable for a fruit with your fat for your afternoon snack, you can do so every other day. For example, spread peanut butter on celery sticks or dip yellow and red pepper strips into hummus.

What's with the sugar-free 10:00 P.M. snacks? For some people, even the taste of refined sugar can be a trigger. If that's you, stick to sugar-free options so you can still be in control of your food. Otherwise, you can have a regular snack instead.

Are you sure I should drink hot chocolate at night? Having something hot and chocolaty that takes a long time to consume is much more satiating than noshing on a small

Kellogg's® Cracklin' Oat Bran®

Nutrition Facts

Serving Size 3/4 Cup (49g/1.8 oz.)
Servings Per Container About 10

Amount Per Serving	Cereal	Cereal with 1/2 Cup Vitamins A&D Fat Free Milk
Calories	200	240
Calories from Fat	60	60
	% Daily Value**	
Total Fat 7g*	**11%**	**11%**
Saturated Fat 3g	**15%**	**15%**
Trans Fat 0g		
Cholesterol 0mg	**0%**	**0%**
Sodium 150mg	**6%**	**9%**
Potassium 220mg	**6%**	**13%**
Total Carbohydrate 35g	**12%**	**14%**
Dietary Fiber 6g	**24%**	**24%**
Sugars 15g		
Other Carbohydrate 14g		
Protein 4g		
Vitamin A	15%	20%
Vitamin C	25%	25%
Calcium	2%	15%
Iron	10%	10%
Vitamin D	10%	25%
Thiamin	25%	30%
Riboflavin	25%	35%
Niacin	25%	25%
Vitamin B6	25%	25%
Folic Acid	25%	25%
Vitamin B12	25%	35%
Phosphorus	15%	25%
Magnesium	15%	20%
Zinc	10%	15%
Copper	8%	10%

* Amount in cereal. One half cup of fat free milk contributes an additional 40 calories, 65mg sodium, 6g total carbohydrates (6g sugars), and 4g protein.
**Percent Daily Values are based on a 2,000 calorie diet. Your daily values may be higher or lower depending on your calorie needs:

	Calories	2,000	2,500
Total Fat	Less than	65g	80g
Saturated Fat	Less than	20g	25g
Cholesterol	Less than	300mg	300mg
Sodium	Less than	2,400mg	2,400mg
Potassium		3,500mg	3,500mg
Total Carbohydrate		300g	375g
Dietary Fiber		25g	30g

Calories per gram: Fat 9 • Carbohydrate 4 • Protein 4

INGREDIENTS: WHOLE OATS, WHEAT BRAN, BROWN SUGAR, PALM OIL, OAT BRAN, CORN SYRUP, SUGAR, COCONUT, MODIFIED WHEAT STARCH, CINNAMON, MALT SYRUP, BAKING SODA, SODIUM ASCORBATE AND ASCORBIC ACID (VITAMIN C), NATURAL AND ARTIFICIAL VANILLA FLAVOR, SALT, NIACINAMIDE, NUTMEG, REDUCED IRON, ZINC OXIDE, PYRIDOXINE HYDROCHLORIDE (VITAMIN B6), RIBOFLAVIN (VITAMIN B2), VITAMIN A PALMITATE, THIAMIN HYDROCHLORIDE (VITAMIN B1), FOLIC ACID, VITAMIN B12 AND VITAMIN D, SOY LECITHIN.

CONTAINS WHEAT AND SOY INGREDIENTS.

Exchange: 2 Carbohydrates, 1 Fat
The dietary exchanges are based on the *Exchange Lists for Meal Planning*, ©2003 by The American Diabetes Association, Inc. and The American Dietetic Association.

Figure 10.1.
Even healthy-sounding foods can be full of sugar and corn syrup.

piece of chocolate—which usually just makes you want the whole bar. If you'd rather not have cocoa, have a hot cup of mint tea with honey and nonfat milk instead. Plan something enjoyable for the night hours when the tendency to binge typically peaks.

What if I'm allergic to nuts? Nuts and nut butters are a great source of healthy fat in small doses. If you can't eat nuts, you can get your fat from healthy oils (olive, sunflower, safflower), seeds (sunflower, flaxseed, wheat germ), or avocados.

You suggest eating shakes for breakfast, but mine always taste terrible! It's usually more satisfying to eat your calories instead of drinking them. You'll feel more satiated by consuming different colors, temperatures, and textures. Sometimes, though, we're in a rush, and grabbing a shake to go is the only option for a protein fix. When making a shake, mix the powder (New PFC makes a great one) with 1 cup of ice and 2 cups of water. The more ice you use, the thicker the shake will be. It's worth investing in a good blender: the shakes taste better and you don't have to replace it frequently.

I feel like I'm eating constantly. How will I ever lose weight? By eating regularly throughout the day, you keep your body at an even keel, giving it what it needs when it needs it to maintain a consistent blood sugar level. When your blood sugar (i.e., insulin) falls, you feel the need to immediately eat something with sugar to raise it again. Once it skyrockets from that dose of sugar, it comes soaring back down, leaving you lethargic and sleepy. Eating regularly eliminates these extreme highs and lows, which only slow down your metabolism.

White flour and sugar tend to spike your blood sugar the most. You'll stay satiated longer having a turkey sandwich on whole-grain bread with mustard and avocado than you would with turkey on white bread with mayo and cheese.

In general, think of your body as a fire. If you throw small pieces of kindling and wood on the fire throughout the day, it'll keep right on roaring. But if you throw on a huge log, it smothers the whole thing out.

I work out for two hours a day, and this amount of food isn't enough for me. If you're still starving after a meal, try adding a little more fat and another half-fist of protein. You should be hungry when it's time to eat, but you don't want to feel homicidal. After eating, you don't want to feel stuffed. You want to feel satisfied and definitely not hungry. Remember, this isn't a diet. It's a nutritional foundation.

I'm worried that I won't be able to control myself on the off day. The off day really works on many levels. Take a glance at your week. If you're going to a big party on Saturday night, make that your off day. Having one day to eat what you like stops you from feeling like you're obsessed with your food and reduces the anxiety that typically accompanies the start of a new plan. It *allows* you a planned time off, avoiding the scenario of finding yourself in the cookie aisle going crazy. You'll find that it's easier to plan out your week and make choices if you know you have some leeway.

If the idea of a whole day with no guidelines makes you feel out of control and as if you'll never get back on track, start by having one to two off meals throughout the week instead. Remember, you might feel temporarily derailed, but one day off can't counteract all your progress. The plan is about making progress for life, not being perfect for one week.

Can I drink caffeine? It's very easy to drink tons of coffee because it can give you a false feeling of energy. But it can also make you act like Oscar the Grouch if you always substitute caffeine for food. One cup a day is fine, but if you desperately need a cup every few hours, take a look at your food intake to see why you aren't getting the energy you need. To cut back on unnecessary fat and calories, save fancy coffee drinks for your off day.

What if I don't want to eat breakfast? Try it anyway. You want to wake up ready to eat so you can get that fire burning. Eating when you wake up keeps your metabolism burning and your energy level up. It's critical to starting your day off on the right foot.

What if I overeat at one meal? It's not the end of the world! Try sticking to protein and veggies for your next meal, and don't beat yourself up about it. Guilt doesn't help anything.

Do I need to worry about sodium? Canned, frozen, or non-fat foods tend to contain a lot of sodium to preserve them and add taste, but sodium leads to bloating. The recommended daily sodium intake is 2,400 mg. Sometimes one frozen dinner can contain a day's worth of sodium! The effects show up in your face, hands, neck, and under your eyes. Even your rings will feel tight.

If you love canned soups, look for low-sodium options or try making some at home. Sodium is also hidden in canned tuna (rinse it off before eating), canned chickpeas, or corn. Even chicken can have hidden sodium.

When you've had a lot of sodium, start drinking water. You won't feel like drinking because you're already so bloated, but the water will flush you out. Stick to foods with high water content, such as a big salad with crunchy veggies or watermelon. Stay away from pastas, breads, and anything with yeast.

I've heard raw veggies are better for you than cooked veggies. Should I stop eating cooked veggies? No way! Yes, raw vegetables have more vitamins and minerals than cooked veggies. But cooked veggies still have tons of health benefits, plus some people with very sensitive tummies do better eating cooked veggies. Don't overdo anything when you don't know how your stomach will respond to it. If you feel gassy, as if your stomach isn't digesting the raw veggies, try steaming them. Even wrapping veggies such as asparagus in foil with olive oil and a little rock salt and barbequing them can be delicious and nutritious.

I'm a vegetarian. Can I still do the S.O.S. plan? Of course! For your protein, try tofu, beans, tempeh, quinoa, and even hemp seeds. Follow the rest of the plan as is.

Are artificial sweeteners OK? Be aware of anything artificial you're putting in your body. When you write your food down in your journal, include how many artificial sweeteners you use.

Do you have just one packet in your morning coffee, or are you using twenty a day and sprinkling it on everything? Sugar-free food options made with artificial sweeteners typically have fewer calories, but your body might not respond as well to them. Pay attention to how you feel, and as with everything, use them in moderation and listen to your body.

What about alcohol? Drink alcohol in moderation. An occasional mixed drink or glass of wine is fine, but if you're drinking a bottle of booze a night, there's bound to be some alcohol weight around your waist.

Alcohol also has lots of sugar in it, which can affect your body negatively. If possible, try to limit your alcohol intake during the week and save it for special occasions. Avoid fancy drinks or anything milky that is high in fat. Stick to lower-calorie and lower-sugar options, such as wine, vodka, and tequila. Mix your drinks with club soda or a splash of juice instead of regular soda.

Can I eat sushi and if so, how much? Sushi is a good mix of protein and carbohydrates, but try to stay away from higher-calorie options such as spicy tuna rolls or tempura rolls. The same portion rules apply to raw fish as to cooked fish. See how many pieces of sashimi would fit in your entire hand (usually about four), and stick to that number.

NO LONGER LOST AT SEA

Say good-bye to overeating, fad diets, and quick fixes that never stick. By adopting the S.O.S. Food Plan as your nutritional foundation, you'll set your food plan on an even keel so you can enjoy the ride. Bon voyage and bon appétit!

Meals, Snacks, and More

11

Conquering Difficult Situations

*I*t's a lot easier to adhere to an eating plan when you have control over every minute of the day. But for most of us, life tends to get in the way. We go to work, we run errands, we date, we travel, we party, and we eat in restaurants. None of these activities have to jeopardize your commitment to the S.O.S. Food Plan. Our tips enable you to maintain a solid nutritional foundation no matter what life throws your way.

EATING OUT

Of course you can still eat at restaurants while following the S.O.S. plan! You might not want to eat out every night, especially in the beginning as you reestablish your nutritional foundation, but the occasional restaurant meal does not have to derail your progress. In fact, feasting on well-prepared protein options can enhance your commitment when you see how tasty good food is! When you follow the S.O.S. Food Plan, you become able to understand your food options and make smarter choices. You learn how to cope with oversized portions and endlessly long menus.

When you eat at a restaurant, *do*:

• **Plan ahead.** Decide what you're going to order before you sit down. Check the restaurant's website for the menu or call ahead for some ideas. Approach your meal with as much information as possible so you don't feel bombarded by options when you get there.

- **Split your meal in half, and ask for the rest of it "to go."** Restaurant portions tend to be extremely large. Ask your server to split your meal in half before it's brought to the table, and take the other half to go. You'll have enough for your next meal and get double your money's worth!

- **Keep the meal basic.** When you look at your plate, you should be able to clearly identify your protein, your vegetables, and your carb. Having everything in a wrap or in a gigantic chopped salad may be confusing or overwhelming, so keep your orders simple.

- **Eat your protein first.** You are more apt to finish your protein if you eat it first. Don't fill up on carbs or veggies. You risk missing out on all the benefits protein has to offer, such as providing energy, helping you build muscle, repairing your cells, and regulating your metabolism.

- **Beware of hidden calories.** Stay away from anything creamed, crispy, fried, or sautéed. Stick to grilled, boiled, roasted, or steamed options, so you don't consume needless empty calories. (Note: stir-fries are still a great option.)

- **Ask for what you need (nicely).** If you're afraid of seeming too high-maintenance when you order, ask yourself what's more important: what the waiter thinks of you or how you'll feel once you've eaten your meal. Ask for dressings and sauces on the side, and don't be afraid to politely send things back if they're not prepared as advertised.

When you eat at a restaurant, *don't*:

- **Devour the bread basket.** If it's too tempting, ask for the waiter to take it away. Order some crudités (i.e., raw veggies) instead.

- **Arrive famished.** Keep in mind that your reservation time is at least thirty minutes before you get your main course. If the restaurant doesn't take reservations, you could be waiting an hour before even sitting down. Have a snack at home or on the way so you don't shovel in the food when it finally arrives. You want to taste and savor your meal, not guzzle it down like a starved animal.

MY GIRL WANTS TO PARTY ALL THE TIME

Pity the poor partier who skulks in the corner, too obsessed with her own body and food to enjoy the people and company around her. Parties are an excuse for celebration and mirth. Even a night at a club can be a memorable (or not!) experience. Try not to let food get in the way of fun. Life is simply too short.

If you're going out on the town, *do*:

- **Eat before you go out.** You don't want to be stranded at a bar or club where your only options are calamari and french fries. Have some protein and a carbohydrate (for example, half a turkey sandwich on whole-grain bread) or a fruit and a fat (such as an apple with peanut butter) before you leave the house. If you know it'll be a superlate night, stash a snack (perhaps almonds) in your purse and make sure to eat again when you start getting hungry.

- **Order low-sugar alcohols.** Opt for vodka and tequila instead of higher-calorie, sugar-laden drinks, such as cosmopolitans and piña coladas.

- **Alternate every drink with a glass of water.** Balancing your water and alcohol intake slows down the effects of alcohol and keeps you hydrated throughout the night.

If you're going out on the town, *don't*:

- **Eat sugar.** Consuming a lot of sugar before going out just makes you sleepy and may give you stinky breath.

- **Consume food that makes you bloated.** Thai, Mexican, and Chinese foods; yeast-filled foods such as pasta; and dairy products all tend to cause gas.

• **Starve yourself all day.** Cutting calories all day and saving them for alcohol at night backfires horribly. You'll be trashed in no time and won't be able to function.

• **Eat whatever's in front of you.** Just because someone else ordered chips and salsa doesn't mean you have to eat them. If you know one handful of chips is a trigger food, avoid it altogether. Order a more benign appetizer, such as a shrimp cocktail. Filling up on empty calories makes you feel like a beached whale instead of the sexy woman you are.

• **Show up unprepared.** Instead of arriving at a dinner party unprepared (and drawing attention to yourself when you don't like any of the meal options), talk to your host ahead of time. Ask him or her what's being served, and nicely explain your food preferences. A good host appreciates your honesty and makes sure to accommodate your requests. You can always eat your protein before you arrive and then just eat the salad and vegetables. Offer to bring a side dish or healthy dessert to help you stay on track. No matter what, don't try to aggressively foist your food plan on anyone else; no one likes to be seated next to an evangelist.

PLANES, TRAINS, AND AUTOMOBILES

Moving around is a fact of life. Whether you're dropping the kids off at school in your minivan or flying to international business meetings on a private jet, you're rarely staying put. Travel doesn't have to be a cause for stress—at least not on the eating front.

If you're traveling, *do*:

• **Pack healthy snacks.** If you're on the road, make sure to pack healthy snacks in a mini-cooler with ice packs that you can keep with you. On planes, avoid the food they give you. Bring on board your own meals and snacks.

• **Be conscious of your travel time.** Just because your expected flight time is fifty-two minutes doesn't mean you'll have a short day of traveling. You have to arrive at the airport early, stand in endless lines, wait for taxi and takeoff, and then wait again for your baggage and transportation. One snack may not cut it. Calculate your minimum travel time, and pack enough to eat every two to three hours.

• **Plan for delays.** If you're stuck in an airport waiting for your delayed flight, make the best of your options. If you didn't have time to pack your own snacks or meals, buy a simple mixed salad from a fast-food restaurant and a grilled chicken breast from another vendor; then chop up the chicken and make yourself a nutritious meal. Grab a piece of fruit and some nuts to tide you over. You never know how long you'll be stuck!

• **Bring your vitamins.** Take Emergen-C, Airborne, or an extra antioxidant-boosting vitamin before boarding a train, bus, or plane to help repel germs.

• **Drink tons of water.** We all tend to retain water when we travel. When flying, try to drink eight ounces of water for every hour you're on the plane. Bring bottled water with you if it's allowed, and focus on cleansing your body throughout the flight. Get up and go to the bathroom as many times as you need to (an aisle seat may help). What else is there to do anyway?

• **Pace yourself.** Whether you're on a cruise confronted by an all-you-can-eat buffet or at a work conference with tables of goodies, pause before you feast. Just because there are a lot of options, doesn't mean you have to eat more than your body needs. Put a few things on your plate, staying consistent with the S.O.S. Food Plan, instead of loading up with everything in sight. Remember, this is not the last time you'll see a buffet—you're not required to try everything on it. If you know buffets make you feel crazy, save them for your off days or research other options before committing to a buffet-only trip. Approach the table with a plan so you can act the way you want.

If you're traveling, *don't*:

• **Drink alcohol or soda.** Doing so just makes you more bloated and dehydrated. Drinks such as Bloody Marys compound the problem because they contain so much salt. Just say no.

• **Succumb to the minibar.** Hotels can inspire you to eat everything in sight. Everything in the minibar seems like a fun surprise, even the regular packet of M&Ms that you could easily buy at a nearby deli for a fraction of the cost but wouldn't. Ask the hotel to clear out the minibar before you arrive. Then run to a local store and buy your own water and snacks (even lemons and limes) for the rest of your stay. You save lots of money, have fewer temptations, and can follow the plan with ease.

- **Fall off the wagon.** Vacation is not an excuse to eat everything in sight. You still have the same body with the same needs—you're just in a different place. Plan to have your one off day, but otherwise stay on track. Vacation can be your own mini-spa-retreat whether you're staying at the Ramada Inn or the Four Seasons. Do your workouts in the mornings and drink tons of water so you can kick back and relax in the afternoons. You won't feel as sluggish, and you'll be less likely to let everything go to hell in a handbasket. Instead of being stressed from an overindulgent trip, arrive home feeling lean and refreshed.

FAD DIET FADE-OUT

*N*ews flash: Quick-fix diets don't work! If a food plan sounds too good to be true, it probably is—even if your favorite celebrity swears by it. There's a reason why many celebrities don't share how they gain and lose weight so quickly for roles: most likely they aren't doing it in the healthiest ways. Some even end up with permanent medical conditions. Don't pick your food plan according to the movie star you like, especially when your body types aren't remotely similar.

Also, when you look at magazines and music videos, remember that the pictures have been *completely* airbrushed. The tabloids make stars look better—or worse—depending on their story that week.

Unfortunately, there's no instant cure for dramatic body transformation. You can't overhaul your body overnight, and a temporary fix isn't going to change your life. You have to learn to manage your life on a daily basis for long-lasting results.

DATING AND RELATIONSHIPS

Dating is stressful enough without adding food to the mix, but don't let meeting Mr. Right overpower your desire to stay fit and fabulous.

When you're on a first date, *do*:

- **Order what you want.** There's a misconception floating out there that men don't like it when women eat. Not true! Men like it when women eat. They *don't* like watching you push a few lettuce leaves around your plate—if they do, run, don't walk, to the nearest exit. If you're tempted to order less than you usually would or feel like your meal seems too big, forget it. The guy could care less as long as you're having fun. He probably won't even remember the restaurant, let alone what you ate, so eat what your body needs.

When you're on a first date, *don't*:

- **Eat foods that make you feel bloated.** Chinese, Thai, Vietnamese, Indian, or Mexican on a date? *No bueno.*

- **Eat to impress.** If you're trying to get to know someone, you have to be yourself. Don't pretend to like foie gras just because he likes it. Stay true to who you are and to your food preferences. If you're already hiding what you like and who you are, you're not being honest with yourself or with him—which will be an exhausting charade to keep up.

When you're in a relationship, *do*:

- **Communicate.** Explain what the S.O.S. Food Plan entails and don't try to hide it. He may decide to come on board and start eating your way. Hopefully, he'll be positive and supportive, which will make life easier for you. The more support you can have around you, the better.

When you're in a relationship, *don't*:

- **Eat the same way he does.** Most likely, you both have different shapes and sizes. Consequently, you need different amounts of fuel to keep your engines running. Just because he likes to eat in a certain way, at a certain time, or a particular type of food doesn't mean you have to.

THE MAIN EVENT

A big event is a great catalyst to change and improve your lifestyle. But it's not just the day of the event that's important. What happens afterward is just as crucial. It's crushing to see a bride-to-be regain those forty pounds, plus another twenty, post-honeymoon.

To avoid this yo-yo trap, figure out what exactly it is or was about the event that motivates you. Was it everyone looking at you? Was it for the pictures? What was it? If you can do it once, you can do it for good. Goals are great, but think long term, not just short term.

OFFICE SPACE

Some jobs don't exactly seem conducive to a lean, livable lifestyle, but that doesn't mean you can't apply the S.O.S. Food Plan tips to transform your work environment.

When you're at work, *do*:

• **Chart out your day.** Plan what time you'll have snacks, drink water, and eat meals. Mark them in your PDA or on your calendar. When you see reminders written there, "3:45 P.M.: Conference call; 4:00 P.M.: Snack," you'll be much more likely to follow it.

• **Stash and grab.** Have a stash of nutritious snacks in your desk or in the communal fridge. If you don't have a communal fridge, buy a mini-fridge to keep in your office or bring your cooler to work.

• **Collect data.** Gather up menus from the places where you order food near the office. Review them at home when you have time or during a lull at work, and then compile a list of meals that will fit with your food plan. If everyone else decides to order out, you'll have your selection ready to go. You can always bring your own lunch to work so that you get exactly what you want. You'll never have to rely on fast food or vending machines again.

• **Timing is everything.** Just because everyone else in the office eats lunch early or late doesn't mean you have to. Eat when you need to, and follow your own plan of attack. You may not always have a long, leisurely lunch break, but you'll fuel your body most appropriately.

When you're at work, *don't*:

• **Get too busy to eat.** We know how crazy the workday can get, but if you forget to eat or push it off, you'll run out of steam before finishing your to-do list. Listen to your body, and follow your set schedule.

SOMETHING BLUE

All of us have bad moods occasionally when we feel sad, lonely, or downright depressed. Getting through them may seem hopeless, but not if you keep this list of tips nearby.

When you're feeling down, *do*:

• **Write.** Set your egg timer for five minutes, grab a pen, and write for five straight minutes about what you're feeling. If you're on a roll, keep writing for as long as you like. It can just be stream-of-consciousness writing, but get it all down. You're not trying to win a Pulitzer Prize. Writing allows you to let go of whatever it is that's upsetting you and will keep you out of the kitchen.

• **Make lists.** When you're upset, it's important to stay grounded and try to put things into perspective. Make a list of twenty things you feel grateful for in your life, even things you take for granted, as minimal or as grand as they seem. Make another list of twenty activities that always make you happy, such as playing with your puppy or taking a warm bath. Then refer back to the lists when you're feeling inconsolable, and do at least one of the happy-making activities you mentioned.

• **Combat boredom.** Feeling bored is often an extension of depression. Find something to do that takes the focus off food. Make a list of your passions, and try to learn something new. Don't let too much time on your hands become too much food in your mouth.

• **Meditate.** Place positive meditation books in the bathroom, and scatter positive quotes around your house. Take time out by popping in a yoga or meditation CD or DVD. Grab a dry erase marker, and write a positive quote on your mirror.

• **Be of service to someone else.** When you're feeling hopeless, pick up the phone and call someone, even if you don't want to. The connection takes the focus off of you and allows you to help someone else. Look up volunteer programs in your neighborhood. Foster an animal, and take it on a walk—great cardio. Work with underprivileged kids. Be creative and make a homemade gift for someone special in your life. Just focus on someone other than yourself.

When you're feeling down, *don't*:

• **Drown your sorrows in food and alcohol.** Nothing you put in your mouth can take away what's on your mind.

• **Keep comfort foods in the house.** Evaluate if you feel comfortable keeping tempting food in the house. If you know you'll eat it when it's there, throw it out or give it away. Don't use your kids as an excuse. Why would you feed them something you wouldn't eat yourself?

EIGHT MILLION THINGS TO DO

Life is nuts. Between work and family, friends and fitness, there's almost no time to pick up the dry cleaning. How can you stay sane—and nourished—in the mayhem?

When you're running errands, *do*:

• **Use a minicooler.** Before you leave, decide how long you'll be gone and pack accordingly. You may need a snack, a meal, and another snack. You'd think to do this for your child, so don't forget to do it for you, too.

• **Change your habits.** If you're used to rewarding yourself with food while doing errands, it's time to make some changes. First, don't run errands when you're hungry (see the previous bullet). Second, if you have certain trigger situations, defuse them. For example, if you always get an ice cream when you pick up prescriptions, switch pharmacies. Third, make your errands enjoyable. Instead of battling it out in the local supermarket, seek out a local farmer's market for fresh produce. Get the dreary tasks done, and then treat yourself to something fun, like a new CD or great magazine.

When you're running errands, *don't*:

• **Fall victim to temptation.** If you know you have to pass your favorite bakery on your way to picking your kids up, do aromatherapy in the car (for example, soak a cotton ball in lavender) or make a hands-free phone call so you won't be sidetracked.

AND THEY'RE OFF . . .

We know. Change isn't always easy. But once you start following our simple fashion, fitness, and nutrition tips, you'll start feeling better about yourself and reaping the benefits immediately. Taking care of yourself causes a wonderful chain reaction. When you start wearing the right clothes for your frame, you'll be even more motivated to work out. When you start working out, you'll want to eat right to properly fuel your body. When you make yourself a priority—your health, your body, your physique—and stick to your positive rhythms, your confidence will soar and your productivity will increase. Others will notice the shift—your transformation will be contagious!

Of course, making lifestyle changes takes time. Be patient. Track your progress along the way, and don't let negative self-talk interfere. Try not to beat yourself up if you get sidetracked. Those downward spirals don't do any good! We don't advocate perfection; every step counts. Just pick up the book again, and start afresh. Dive into a new body part chapter, or try another fashion tip. One little behavior change will put you back on the path to a lean, livable lifestyle. Focus on the journey, not the destination, and you'll be there before you know it. We all have to take our own paths in life. Let our words be your touchstone as you go forward, newly empowered.

Appendix A

Calculating Your BMI

While many websites offer instant body mass index (BMI) calculators, you can still compute your BMI manually by the following method:

1. Multiply your height in inches by your height in inches.
2. Divide your weight in pounds by Step 1.
3. Multiply Step 2 by 703.

For example, if you were 5 feet 6 inches (66 inches) and weighed 140 pounds:

1. Multiply 66 by 66: 66 × 66 = 4,356
2. Divide 140 by 4,356: 140 ÷ 4,356 = 0.0321
3. Multiply 0.0321 by 703: 0.0321 × 703 = 22.59

Your BMI would be 22.6, and you would be a normal weight.

BMI Range
If your BMI is 18.5 or less, you are *underweight*.
If your BMI is between 18.5 and 24.9, you are of a *normal weight*.
If your BMI is between 25 and 29.9, you are *overweight*.
If your BMI is 30 or more, you are *obese*.

Charting Your Body Measurements

Body Part	Week						
	1	3	5	7	9	11	13
Neck							
Chest							
Waist							
Abs							
Hips							
Right arm, relaxed							
Left arm, relaxed							
Right arm, flexed							
Left arm, flexed							
Quads							
Thighs							
Calves							

Appendix C

Goal Worksheet

Use this worksheet to write out your goals every week.

Date: _____

Physical: These goals relate to your level of physical activity. For example, "I commit to three 45-minute sessions of fat-burning cardio a week for the next two weeks."

Goal #1: _____
Goal #2: _____
Goal #3: _____

Emotional: These goals relate to how you let (or don't let) your emotions affect your eating. For example, "Instead of stopping at Baskin-Robbins and eating ice cream when I get fed up with work, I'll go home and e-mail a friend."

Goal #1: _____
Goal #2: _____
Goal #3: _____

Behavioral: These goals relate to actions you can take to improve your well-being. For example, "I will prepare my food on Sunday and Wednesday for the upcoming week."

Goal #1: _____

Goal #2: _____

Goal #3: _____

Nutritional: These goals relate to your food intake. For example, "I will eat a fruit with a fat for my two snacks each day."

Goal #1: _____

Goal #2: _____

Goal #3: _____

Food Journal

Use this worksheet to record your intake and corresponding feelings for at least eleven consecutive days.

Meal 1 Time: _____ Water: _____ Feeling: _____
_____
_____

Meal 2 Time: _____ Water: _____ Feeling: _____
_____
_____

Meal 3 Time: _____ Water: _____ Feeling: _____
_____
_____

Meal 4 Time: _____ Water: _____ Feeling: _____
_____
_____

Meal 5 Time: _____ Water: _____ Feeling: _____
_____
_____

Meal 6 Time: _____ Water: _____ Feeling: _____

_____
_____
_____

Cardio and training:

_____
_____
_____

Appendix E

Nutrition List

Note: the portion sizes listed are for reference only. See Chapter 10 for recommended portion sizes on the S.O.S. plan. The following information applies to raw veggies only.

Colorful Vegetables	Portion Size	Calories	Protein (g)	Carb (g)	Fat (g)
Alfalfa sprouts	3 cups	30	3.96	3.78	0.6
Asparagus	1 cup	30	4.1	4.9	0.3
Beets	½ cup	30	1	6.6	0.1
Broccoli	1 cup	24	2.6	3	0.06
Brussels sprouts	1 cup	38	3.3	7.8	0.26
Cabbage	2 cups	32	1.68	5.5	0.2
Carrot juice	⅓ cup	32	0.8	7.3	0
Carrots	½ cup	24	0.5	5.5	0.1
Cauliflower	1 cup	24	1.9	4.9	0.18
Celery	2 cups	36	1.6	8.72	0.28
Chard, Swiss	4 cups	24	2.56	5.3	0.3
Collard greens	1 cup	35	2.9	7	0.4
Cucumbers	2 cups	28	1.12	6	0.28
Eggplants	1 cup	22	0.9	5	0.08
Endive	4 cups	24	2.4	6.7	0.4
Green beans	1 cup	34	2	7.8	0.01
Kale	1 cup	33	2.21	6.7	0.47
Leeks	½ cup	38	0.9	8.7	0.18

Colorful Vegetables	Portion Size	Calories	Protein (g)	Carb (g)	Fat (g)
Lettuce, iceberg	3 cups	30	0.21	6.6	0.36
Lettuce, romaine	3 cups	24	2.7	3.9	0.36
Mung bean sprouts	1 cup	32	3	6	0.2
Mushrooms	2 cups	36	2.9	6	0.4
Okra	1 cup	38	2	7.6	0.1
Onions, green	1 cup	26	1.7	5.5	0.14
Onions, mature	½ cup	25	0.64	5.85	0.21
Parsley	1 cup	26	2.2	5.1	0.4
Peppers, chili	½ cup	30	1.5	7	0.15
Peppers, sweet	1 cup	26	2.2	5.1	0.4
Pumpkin	½ cup	25	0.88	6	0.08
Sauerkraut	1 cup	42	2.4	9.4	0.33
Spinach, raw	2 cups	28	3.6	4.8	0.4
Squash, summer	1 cup	25	1.4	5.5	0.28
Tomatoes	1	24	1.1	5.3	0.26
Turnips	1 cup	39	1.3	8.6	0.13

Carby Vegetables	Portion Size	Calories	Protein (g)	Carb (g)	Fat (g)
Artichokes	1 med	65	3.4	15.3	0.26
Chickpeas (garbanzo beans)	¼ cup	67	3.65	11.25	1.05
Corn	½ cup	66	2.48	14.5	0.9
Peas, green	½ cup	59	3.95	10.5	0.29
Peas, split	⅓ cup	77	5.3	13.8	0.1
Potatoes	½ cup	57	1.6	12.85	0.1
Potatoes, baked	⅓ potato	73	1.3	10.9	0.06
Squash, winter	½ cup	68	1	16	0.19
Sweet potatoes	½ potato	68	1	16	0.19
Yams	⅓ cup	70	1.6	16	0.13

Vegetable Soups	Portion Size	Calories	Protein (g)	Carb (g)	Fat (g)
Black bean soup	1 cup	116	5.64	19.8	1.51
Gazpacho	1 cup	57	8.69	0.78	2.24

Vegetable Soups	Portion Size	Calories	Protein (g)	Carb (g)	Fat (g)
Minestrone	1 cup	83	4.26	11.2	2.51
Tomato	1 cup	86	2.06	16.6	1.92
Vegetable	1 cup	72	2.1	12	1.93

Fruit	Portion Size	Calories	Protein (g)	Carb (g)	Fat (g)
Apple juice	½ cup	58	0.07	14.5	0.14
Apples	1 med.	81	0.25	21	0.49
Applesauce	½ cup	53	0.2	13.75	0.06
Bananas	1	105	1.8	26.7	0.55
Blackberries	1 cup	74	1.04	18.3	0.56
Cantaloupe	½ melon	94	2.34	22.3	0.54
Gooseberries	1 cup	67	1.32	15.2	0
Grapefruit	1	76	1.5	19.4	0.24
Grapefruit juice	½ cup	48	0.62	11.35	0.13
Grapes	1 cup	58	0.58	15.7	0.32
Guava	2	90	1.43	20.4	0.7
Honeydew melon	⅙ melon	76.7	0.98	19.7	0.22
Kiwifruit	2	92	1.5	22.6	0.68
Mangoes	½ mango	67.5	0.53	17.5	0.28
Mulberries	1 cup	61	2.02	13.7	0.55
Nectarines	1	67	1.28	16	0.54
Orange juice	½ cup	55	0.87	12.9	0.25
Oranges	1	62	1.23	15.4	0.15
Papaya	½ papaya	59	0.93	15	0.21
Passion fruit	4	72	1.6	16.84	0.52
Peaches	2 small	74	1.22	19.3	0.16
Pears	1	98	0.65	25	0.66
Persimmon	½ persimmon	59	0.49	15.6	0.15
Pineapple	1 cup	77	0.6	19.2	0.66
Pineapple juice	½ cup	69.5	0.4	17.2	0.1
Plantain, raw or cooked	½ cup	90	0.96	23.6	0.27
Plums	2 small	72	1.04	17.18	0.62

Fruit	Portion Size	Calories	Protein (g)	Carb (g)	Fat (g)
Prickly pear	2	84	1.5	18.7	0.53
Prune juice	½ cup	90	0.77	22.3	0.04
Prunes	3	60	0.65	15.81	0.12
Raisins	⅛ cup	61	0.69	12.15	0.15
Raspberries	1 cup	61	1.11	14.2	0.68
Rhubarb, raw	3 cups	78	3.27	16.5	0.72
Strawberries	1½ cups	67.5	1.36	15.6	0.62
Tangerine juice	½ cup	52	0.62	12.5	0.24
Tangerines	2	74	1.06	18.8	0.32
Watermelon	1 cup	50	0.99	11.5	0.68

Carb: Beans, Cooked	Portion Size	Calories	Protein (g)	Carb (g)	Fat (g)
Black	⅓ cup	59	4.4	9.9	0.4
Kidney	⅓ cup	72	4.8	13.2	0.3
Lima	⅓ cup	69	3.8	13	0.18
Navy	⅓ cup	74	4.9	13.4	0.36

Carb: Grains (in Moderation)	Portion Size	Calories	Protein (g)	Carb (g)	Fat (g)
Cracked-wheat bread	1 slice	60	2	12	0.6
English muffin (whole grain)	½ muffin	65	2.2	12	0.5
Macaroni	½ cup	76	2.4	16.1	0.5
Mixed-grain bread	1 slice	51.4	1.9	9.3	0.7
Pancakes (whole grain or buckwheat)	4-inch diameter	54	1.8	6.4	2.15
Pasta	1 oz.	100	5	19.5	0.25
Pita, whole wheat	½ pita	70	3	12	1
Pumpernickel bread	1 slice	79	2.9	17	0.4
Rolls, whole wheat	1	90	3.5	18.3	1
Spaghetti	½ cup	77.5	2.4	16.1	0.3
Tortilla, corn	6-inch diameter	63	1.5	13.5	0.6
Whole-wheat bread	1 slice	56	2.4	11	0.7

Carb: Cereal	Portion Size	Calories	Protein (g)	Carb (g)	Fat (g)
Cream of rice	½ cup	62	1	14.2	0
Cream of wheat	½ cup	67	1.9	13.85	0.25
Corn grits	½ cup	73	1.75	15.7	0.25
Oat flakes	½ cup	89	2.65	10.25	0.2
Oat puffs	¾ cup	55	1.25	11.7	0.35
Oatmeal	½ cup	72.5	3	12.6	1.2
Rice, puffed	1 cup	56	0.9	12.6	0.1
Wheat, granules (Grape-Nuts)	¼ cup	101	3.3	23.2	0.1
Wheat, puffed	1 cup	44	1.8	9.5	0.1
Wheat, shredded	1 large	83	2.6	18.8	0.3

Carb	Portion Size	Calories	Protein (g)	Carb (g)	Fat (g)
Lentils	⅓ cup	70	5.2	12.8	0
Rice, brown	⅓ cup	78.2	1.64	16.8	0.4
Rice, white	⅓ cup	78.6	1.46	17.4	0.17
Rice, wild	⅓ cup	63	2.5	13.4	0.28

Protein: Soy	Portion Size	Calories	Protein (g)	Carb (g)	Fat (g)
Soybean curd (tofu)	3½ oz.	72	7.8	2.4	4.2
Soybean milk	1 cup	75	7.7	5	3.4
Tofu, firm	2 oz.	82	9	2.4	5

Protein: Fish	Portion Size	Calories	Protein (g)	Carb (g)	Fat (g)
Bass	2 oz.	54.6	10	0	0.6
Bluefish	2 oz.	70	11.2	0	2.4
Catfish	2 oz.	66	10.2	0	2.4
Cod	2 oz.	46.6	10	0	0.38
Flatfish (sole, flounder)	2 oz.	52	10.6	0	0.6
Haddock	2 oz.	49.4	10.8	0	0.2
Mackerel	1 oz.	58	5.9	0	3.9
Salmon	1 oz.	40.3	5.6	0	1.7

Protein: Fish	Portion Size	Calories	Protein (g)	Carb (g)	Fat (g)
Snapper	2 oz.	56.6	11.6	0	0.76
Swordfish	2 oz.	56.6	11.2	0	2.2
Trout	2 oz.	84	11.8	0	3.7
Tuna (in water)	2 oz.	72	16.2	0	2.7
White fish	2 oz.	76	10.6	0	3.2

Protein: Poultry	Portion Size	Calories	Protein (g)	Carb (g)	Fat (g)
Chicken, white, skinless	1 oz.	33	6.8	0	0.48
Turkey, white	1 oz.	44	6	0	2

Protein: Beef	Portion Size	Calories	Protein (g)	Carb (g)	Fat (g)
Beef tenderloin	1 oz.	68	5.2	0	5.1
Flank steak	1 oz.	56	5.4	0	3.5
Ground beef	1 oz.	74.5	5	0	5.8
Round steak	1 oz.	68	5.5	0	4.9
Sirloin steak	1 oz.	74	5.17	0	5.7

Protein: Eggs	Portion Size	Calories	Protein (g)	Carb (g)	Fat (g)
Egg whites	3	48	10.05	1.23	0
Whole egg	1	79	6.07	0.6	5.58

Fats: Nuts and Seeds	Portion Size	Calories	Protein (g)	Carb (g)	Fat (g)
Almonds	12 nuts	106.1	3.3	3.4	9.6
Cashews	12 nuts	114.5	2.5	1.9	11.7
Hazelnuts	12 nuts	107	2.12	2.8	10.5
Peanuts	12 nuts	104.7	4.7	3.7	8.7
Pumpkin seeds	⅛ cup	96.7	5	2.6	8.1
Sesame seeds	⅛ cup	109	3.4	3.3	10
Sunflower seeds	⅛ cup	101	4.3	3.6	8.5

Fats: Oils	Portion Size	Calories	Protein (g)	Carb (g)	Fat (g)
Avocado	⅓ avocado	108	1.33	4.9	10.2
Olive oil	1 tbsp.	119	0	0	13.5
Peanut oil	1 tbsp.	119	0	0	13.5
Safflower oil	1 tbsp.	120	0	0	13.6
Wheat germ	1 tbsp.	120	0	0	13.6

Miscellaneous	Portion Size	Calories	Protein (g)	Carb (g)	Fat (g)
Chives	1 tbsp.	1	0.08	0.1	0.02
Garlic	1 clove	4	0.2	0.9	0.02
Pickles, dill	1 large	11	0.7	2.2	0.4
Pimientos	1 med.	9	0.3	1.9	0.16
Radish	10	7	0.8	1.1	0.04
Watercress	1 cup	7	0.8	1.1	0.04

Beverages	Portion Size	Calories	Protein (g)	Carb (g)	Fat (g)
Beer	12 oz.	148	0.94	13.2	0
Coffee (plain)	6 oz.	3	0	0.54	0.01
Gin, rum, whiskey, vodka	1 oz.	70	0	0	0
Wine, red	3½ oz.	76	0.21	2.52	0
Wine, white	3½ oz.	80	0.15	3.4	0

Grapendix F

Grocery List

Carbohydrates

Black beans
Cereal: Optimum, Fiber One, Shredded Wheat (large size)
Chickpeas (garbanzo beans)
Cream of wheat or cream of rice
Oatmeal: Quaker slow-cooked or instant packets
Rice: slow-cooked or instant (brown or white)
Seven-grain fresh-made bread or any whole-grain bread
   that does not have partially hydrogenated oil in the
   ingredients
Whole-wheat and/or brown rice tortillas

Fruits

Fresh

Apples (Fuji apples are very sweet.)
Bananas
Berries (e.g., blueberries, strawberries, raspberries—frozen
   optional)
Oranges
Pineapple

Canned

Any fruit that says "no sugar added"
Applesauce, little plastic cup to go, natural—no sugar added
Pineapple, pop-top, no sugar added (Motts, Dole)

Vegetables

Artichokes
Asparagus
Broccoli
Cabbage, purple
Carrots
Corn
Cucumbers
Hearts of palm
Lettuce: heads or bags (The darker the lettuce,
     the more iron it has.)
Onions
Peas (any kind)
Peppers, all colors
Squash
Tomatoes
White potatoes
Yams and sweet potatoes

Proteins

Chicken or turkey breast, skinless
Deli turkey or chicken (Honey roasted is tasty. Have the deli
     separate into ¼-pound sections with wax paper. It makes
     it easier to grab the correct portion.)
Eggs, free range
Flank steak
Ground beef, turkey, or chicken
Halibut
Protein powder (newpfc.com: whey protein powder)
Salmon
Sea bass
Sole or flounder
Tuna, canned, in water (Rinse it.)
White fish

Fat

Almonds
Avocado
Cashews
Hazelnuts
Natural peanut, cashew, or hazelnut butter
Olive oil
Peanuts
Pumpkin seeds
Sesame seeds
Sunflower seeds
Wheat germ (Kretschmer)

Miscellaneous

Balsamic vinegar
Cinnamon
Coffee
Green tea
Hot chocolate (sugar free)
Lemon
Lime
Mrs. Dash's spices
Multivitamins
Mustard
Pepper
Salsa
Salt
Sugar-free chocolate ice pops
Udo's Oil Blend (florahealth.com): An excellent source of omega 3, 6, and 9 fatty acids, and flax, sunflower, and evening of primrose oils. It is great for promoting a lean physique, great skin, and healthy hair. Udo's can be purchased in the refrigerated vitamin section of your local health food store (e.g., Whole Foods). One tablespoon per 50 pounds of body weight. It can be mixed with food or consumed on its own, but chase it with a sip of juice. Do half in the morning and half at night or break it up throughout the day.

Resources

Paige Premium Denim Store
116 N. Robertson Blvd.
Los Angeles, CA 90048
(310) 360-9888
paigepremiumdenim.com

National Eating Disorders Association (NEDA)
603 Stewart St., Suite 803
Seattle, WA 98101
(206) 382-3587
Referral helpline: (800) 931-2237
nationaleatingdisorders.org

Udo Erasmus, Ph.D., nutrition
udoerasmus.com

Matt Mahowald, nutrition
newpfc.com

Karl List, fitness
karllist.com

Overeaters Anonymous
oa.org

Ashley Borden Fitness and Lifestyle
8205 Santa Monica Blvd., #1-479
West Hollywood, CA 90046
(310) 499-6037
ashleyborden.com

Index

About the Authors

Paige Adams-Geller (paigepremiumdenim.com) grew up in Wasilla, Alaska, where she was exposed to the glamorous world of pageants at an early age. At sixteen, she was offered a contract by a modeling agency in New York City (Elite Models). Adams-Geller left the modeling world after developing anorexia nervosa and a lasting struggle with body image.

Adams-Geller moved to Los Angeles to attend the University of Southern California where she graduated with a degree in communications and joined the entertainment scene once more as Miss California in 1991. As she was still struggling with body image and a gripping eating disorder, Adams-Geller went through treatment where she was encouraged to focus on a career outside of the entertainment business. Joining the world of fit modeling, she became the "it girl" for designer denim and quickly became known as "the best butt in the business." Learning to embrace her natural curves, Adams-Geller believes that all body types should be considered in fashion design, which inspired her to launch her own line in 2004 that focused on a great fit, comfort, and style. Paige Premium Denim was born and sailed to success, becoming one of the top-selling brands across the globe in less than three years.

Adams-Geller resides in Los Angeles with her husband, two stepchildren, and canine companions Taffy and Ashley.

Ashley Borden (ashleyborden.com) is a fitness and lifestyle consultant to some of Hollywood's most recognizable faces. Her unique approach to fitness can be attributed to how she tackled her own personal struggles and transformed them into a positive philosophy and dynamic training program—making her one of the most sought-after experts in her field. Her personality and humor suits all types of celebrity clients, including Christina Aguilera, Mandy Moore, Chaka Khan, Penny Marshall, Sean Hayes, Tori Spelling, Poppy Montgomery, Annabeth Gish, Lauren Graham, and top professional athletes.

Ashley's tips and techniques have been featured in *InStyle*, *Vogue*, *Shape*, *Self*, *Cosmopolitan*, *Harper's Bazaar*, and *Glamour*, to name just a few. She is also a selected member of *Fitness* magazine's advisory board. Internationally, Borden has been recognized by publications such as *Elle Japan*, Australia's *Who Weekly*, and London's *NOW* magazine. In addition, she is a resident fitness and lifestyle expert on the "Tyra Banks Show" and has been interviewed on the "Today Show," Discovery Health, MTV, VH1, E!, and more.

Borden is a Nike Elite Fitness Professional, a L.I.S.T. master trainer, and is certified with the National Health Club Association. You can train with her at podfitness.com—the largest resource for downloading customized fitness programs for iPods and MP3s or in West Hollywood, California, where she privately trains her clients.

Freelance writer Zibby Right (zibbyright.com) has contributed to numerous publications, including *Self*, *Shape*, *Seventeen*, *Modern Bride*, and *Elegant Bride*. She is a contributing editor for *Quest* and the coeditor in chief of *The Insider's Guide to the Colleges*, *1999*. A graduate of Harvard Business School and Yale University, Right lives with her husband, twins, and bulldog in Manhattan.